"...it is easier to sail many thousand miles through cold and storm and cannibals, in a government ship, with five hundred men and boys to assist one, than it is to explore the private sea, the Atlantic and Pacific Ocean of one's being alone."

—HENRY DAVID THOREAU, Walden

THE PRIVATE SEA

THE PRIVATE SEA

LSD and the search for God

by William Braden

Quadrangle Books, Chicago

To my wife Beatrice, who summed up the contemporary condition better than anybody else perhaps when she observed: *"Cogito, ergo sum—cogito."* I also liked her reply to the fellow who declared, "To understand all is to forgive all." Said she: "How do you know?"

Acknowledgments

I should like to express my gratitude to the *Chicago Sun-Times* for permission to reuse materials contained in articles which I wrote for that newspaper. For encouraging me to write the articles, I should like to thank my editors at the *Sun-Times*— especially Emmett Dedmon, Ralph Otwell, and James F. Hoge, Jr. For invaluable assistance in the preparation of this manuscript, my sincere thanks go also to Robert J. Burdett and John R. Mahon. Finally, for reading the manuscript and for many helpful suggestions, I am very grateful to Dr. Martin E. Marty and Dr. Joseph M. Kitagawa of the University of Chicago Divinity School.

Contents

THE PRIVATE SEA

1 The pearl of great price

At a party in Chicago, a young man under the influence of LSD seized a live kitten and ate it. Later, in an effort to explain his action, he said he had felt an urgent need to experience everything.

The story is revolting, of course, and possibly apocryphal; but the incident is by no means improbable, and it does make the point—that LSD is powerful medicine, and that the consequences of its use are often bizarre and terrifying. While it now appears that health authorities have exaggerated the threat of self-destruction or mental breakdown, the fact remains that LSD is dangerous. The nature of the danger, however, may be other than is commonly supposed, and it is possible the alarmists are not nearly as alarmed as they should be. Almost anything may happen when LSD produces the negative reaction that inner-space voyagers refer to as a "bad trip," and such a reaction is by no means uncommon; but LSD also can result in a good trip, which is more to the point, and the good trip may in the long run have graver consequences than the bad. Indeed, there are implications in the use of LSD which are far more disturbing perhaps than an occasional suicide or psychosis.]

Assume just for a moment that LSD's cultists are actually doing what they suppose they are doing. If you can take their own word for it, they have been tinkering with the gears of the universe. They have rushed in where Sigmund Freud feared to tread, invading a region of the human psyche from which the father of psychoanalysis recoiled in horror. They have penetrated a realm of Egyptian darkness—courageously, perhaps, or recklessly it may be—and in doing so they have raised fundamental questions about man and God.

Whatever the answers, the questions are valid. They are not new questions but very old ones, and some have their roots in a philosophical tradition which predates Western civilization. LSD has merely given them a renewed emphasis.

Moreover, the LSD cults are not an isolated phenomenon. There is some evidence that they represent only one aspect of a psychic revolt whose manifestations can be detected today in the areas of theology, psychology, and ethics. For example, the cults appear to have a relationship to the radical New Theology, and especially to the ultra-radical Death of God theology. In essence, the LSD cultists are saying the same thing that some of the Death of God prophets have said.

From one point of view, LSD presents the orthodox church with a challenge more awesome than the Turk and the comet— from which, good Lord, deliver us. It casts doubt on the validity of religious experience as a whole, suggesting that the mystical awareness of God is nothing more than chemistry—and therefore a delusion. From another point of view, however, the drug raises just as many questions for the atheist as it does for the church. It challenges the scientist as well as the priest. And some of its more extravagant enthusiasts believe it will lead the way to a rebirth of the spirit—to a new Age of Faith in which man's soul in the twentieth century will win an ultimate victory over materialism and a skeptical science.

Its members in fact have described the drug movement as religious—if not a religion—and some groups already have incorporated as churches. But if there is to be a new age, there also will be a new faith, for the LSD cultists in many cases are promulgating concepts which basically are alien to popular Western theology. Perhaps the most striking aspect of the New Theology has been its re-emphasis of the concept of *immanence*, or the indwelling nature of God—as opposed to *transcendence*, or the "otherness" of God. While immanence as such is by no means heretical, in the drug movement and in Death of God theology immanence is carried all the way to its radical conclusion, where it becomes pantheism. Pantheism of course is an Eastern concept, and the West has regarded it as anathema, describing it invariably as "a vague pantheism"—as opposed presumably to such crystal-clear doctrines as transubstantiation and trinitarianism. But pantheism is not vague. Whatever the merits of the idea, it is perfectly clear-cut and straightforward in its assertion: *God is Man.* Or God is the Universe. There is nothing very complicated about that, and that is pantheism. It is, by and large, the Eastern view of divinity. By and large, it represents the direction in which the drug movement appears to be headed. And, in so many words, it sums up the position of the theological school represented by Dr. Thomas J. J. Altizer.

When Altizer says God is Dead, he means simply that God is Man. Altizer is a pantheist, and he admits he is a pantheist. His pantheism is not quite the same as the Eastern version, as we shall see further on; but it is nonetheless pantheism and basically therefore an Oriental concept. In this respect, along with LSD, it hints at a development that could have considerable significance for Western society.

East is still East, and West is still West, but there is evidence now that the twain have started to meet, and at a point where one might least have expected it: the point of religious metaphysics. It appears that there is presently occurring, especially in America, a wholesale introduction of Asian theories regarding the nature of man and the cosmos. This development began long ago, in a small way, in the New England of Emerson and Thoreau, but it seems to have accelerated tremendously since the Second World War. Sages throughout history have prophesied the day when the Wise Men of the Orient would join hands—or lock horns—with the Wise Men of the Occident, and signs abound that the day has arrived as a natural consequence of the shrinking of the globe. In a sense, the immanent God of the East has come knocking at the door of the transcendent God of the West, and it is possible that we are witnesses today to a kind of cosmic shoot-out at the O.K. Corral. It would be premature to assess the full impact of the encounter or its likely denouement, but there seems to be little doubt that the encounter is taking place and that certain fundamentals of Eastern thought are being integrated or assimilated into Western culture. In its initial stages the development preceded both radical theology and the drug movement; but it is obvious that these are related to the development, just as they are related to each other, and it would be worthwhile perhaps to judge them at least partially within this wider context.

Within such a context, LSD and the Death of God oppose orthodoxy in crucial areas of doctrine. Not only do they dispute the idea of Theism, or a personal and transcendent deity, but they also question such concepts as pluralism, resurrection, personal immortality, grace, evil, and redemption or atonement through the intercession of some supernatural agency. In short, they leave man pretty much on his own, with nobody to turn to but himself and with no place to seek salvation except inwardly, in the recesses of his own inner Being. Putting these doctrinal concerns to one side, the drug movement challenges the church in its functional role as well. According to the LSD cultists, men today are thirsting for the direct, personal experience of God— regardless of his actual nature. In other words, it matters not whether God lies within or without; in either case, men need and want a sense of direct communion with the ultimate source of their faith. This divine-human encounter is not found in church, where little or nothing is done to promote it. But it is found in LSD, the cultists believe. Thus LSD challenges the church to do as well and offer as much.

The debate spills over into the province of psychology, where a related movement is under way to establish standards of behavior and adaptation based on universal truths rather than social norms. Mental health would be defined in terms of man's actual nature or Being, and LSD might prove a helpful tool in determining what that nature or Being really is. Such a program of course would introduce psychology to the field of values and ethics, which many have argued is a field that psychology should have occupied long before now. And it might open the way to the development of a humanistic morality founded on man's true nature, replacing those legalistic moralities which are founded on cultural mores or instinctive but arbitrary notions of right and wrong. Coincidentally, this movement comes at a time when psychoanalysts are doing their best to repress a theory that schizophrenia is a physical disease, best treated by massive doses of Vitamin B-3. The theory reduces Freud more or less to the status of a witch doctor, and it raises the possibility at least of a common origin for insanity, religious mysticism, and LSD experience.

It may be that all of these movements are interrelated in still another fashion, reflecting a revived interest in the study of metaphysics—and especially that branch of metaphysics termed ontology, or the metaphysics of Being: the study of life's essential nature. Academic philosophy had largely abandoned metaphysics in favor of an arcane linguistic analysis, and churchmen for the most part had turned their attention to such mundane considerations as ecumenicism, internal renewal, and civil rights. Now it appears that metaphysics has come into its own again—both inside the church and out of it, but mostly out of it, and not so much yet in the universities. And this is just a fancy way of saying that people have started once more to ask ultimate questions. They are asking who they are, and who God is, and what is the relationship, if any, between them and him. Altizer is asking these questions, and so is the hipster who seeks cosmic fireworks in an LSD sugar cube. They are asking the questions that Gauguin asked on his canvas: "Where Do We Come From? What Are We? Where Are We Going?" It might be said that men have found themselves confronted by two kinds of questions, problems and mysteries. In recent years, men have dealt primarily with the problems; but the mysteries are now and always will be the source of the world's essential anxieties and aspirations, and it appears that men are probing afresh into the mysteries, including the *mysterium tremendum*. They are seeking again the pearl of great price.

The asking of ultimate questions is significant in itself. It implies an assumption that there are ultimate answers, and that these answers moreover are accessible to men. In recent times, it seems fair to say, this assumption has not been widely held or widely expressed. Even proud science has gone mute on the subject, having painted itself into that corner known as Heisenberg's Principle of Uncertainty. As a result, it has been said, the very best we can hope for apparently is that science one day will be able to describe everything—and explain nothing. But the new search for answers is not predicated upon scientific principles, nor indeed is it predicated upon orthodox religious principles; it seems to reject both the Scribes and the Pharisees, the scientists and the formal religionists. If it does in fact constitute a religious revival, which is open to argument, it is one which is bypassing the church's magisterium. It is eclectic, and it rejects all outward authority. On the other hand, it does accept the basic religious premise, as William James defined it: "the belief that there is an unseen order, and that our supreme good lies in harmoniously adjusting ourselves thereto." Fundamentally, today's pearl seekers are following Plato's injunction. They are striving for an explanation of Being, which all true lovers of knowledge must have as their final object, Plato said. They are inquiring into the nature of their own Being and into the nature of Being itself. And they are conducting the inquiry by turning inward upon themselves, like flowers closing their

21

petals in the night of doubt. Like poppies, one might add, or possibly morning glories and lotuses. But that is another question.

All in all, the challenge appears to be directed toward the laboratory more than the pulpit. The implications of the drug movement are basically anti-science rather than anti-church, and they offer grounds for some far-reaching speculation. We spoke earlier of a possible psychic revolt, and we might ask whether this is not in fact suggested now by the widespread interest in LSD and by related developments in radical theology and psychology. Are these perhaps omens of a counter-swing of the psychic pendulum? Over the centuries, as the classical historian Edith Hamilton has observed, that pendulum has swung back and forth: from the rational to the intuitive, from the seen to the unseen, from the conscious to the unconscious. Whenever one alternative has failed to answer man's questions or to meet his needs, he has turned invariably to the other option; it follows, therefore, that the apparent challenge now is not merely to science but to rational thought as such. And this is necessarily so. It can be argued that the erosion of religious belief has not been caused so much by the specific revelations of science; rather, it is a result of the empirical method which science has utilized to obtain those revelations—of the introduction into the culture of a show-me frame of reference which might be characterized as the Missouri Syndrome. If empiricism has proved a disappointment, as indeed it has, it is entirely possible that the instinctive and unconscious forces of the mind may be rising again now in opposition to the rational and the conscious; the spiritual element may be reasserting itself in an era when scientific rationalism had appeared to be solidly entrenched. An outburst of mysticism perhaps has been simmering on the rear burner for some time, in fact, and, if you care to, you might trace the possibility back to the anti-rational philosophy of Henri Bergson.

Now LSD has turned up the flame.

Of course, a revolt is not a revolution. The flame could die—from lack of oxygen—and empiricism may be just as impregnable as it thought it was. But the movements of the time deserve serious attention even if they do not, for the moment, seem to be leading anywhere or offering much substance. What men search for, after all, is just as significant in a sense as that which they find, providing some measure at least of their nature and their needs.

But suppose the revolt did ripen into a revolution. Would that necessarily be a bad thing? What, if any, are the dangers involved?

The main danger, already apparent, is the possibility that these various movements could lead to a sort of neo-Gnostic rejection of the world—a retreat from the concrete, as it were, resulting in the kind of pipe-dream lethargy which characterizes so much of India and the Middle East, and which is symbolized in turn by the Hindu contemplative and the Arab hashish-eater: the one held spellbound by an idea, the other by a drug. And perhaps the gravest challenge is not after all to science, or to rationalism, but to the world as such. Not just the values of the world, not just social goals, but the world itself, as earth and substance. The danger in this case arises from Oriental concepts of the world as some kind of illusion, trick, or snare for the senses. According to this point of view, the world does not really exist. It's all done with mirrors, and the purpose of life is to realize this fact, such realization bringing with it an immediate release from the world where man is held captive by his own ignorance. Upon such release the enlightened one attains the eternal bliss of nirvana, beyond appearances.

What we have called a danger—and the Hindu calls a blessing—is not a problem in so far as radical theology is concerned. New Theology is utterly committed to the world, having turned away from the heavens, and Death of God theology actually rejoices in the world, embraces it, cherishes it, and does all but make love to it. Contrary to their popular image, the Death of God people are by and large a jolly and optimistic lot. As the radical theologian William Hamilton expressed it, in so many words: Prufrock, no; Ringo, yes. As far as he is concerned, the Wasteland has been transformed into a latter-day Canaan. Man is no longer alienated from the world, according to Hamilton. Man is "quite at home in this world." And next to Altizer, Hamilton is a gloomy Gus. All this happy talk stems directly from the fact that God is no longer around to spoil the fun, so to speak.

The danger of world rejection exists within the drug movement, where one hears cultists referring to the Net of Illusion and the Quagmire of Phenomena. But even if you grant the basic validity of the drug experience, it does not necessarily follow that the world is a hoax. After all, there are Oriental philosophies and Oriental philosophies. The Hindu and the Zen Buddhist start from the same point of view; they share a common experience, and they argue from the same evidence. But they arrive at antipodal conclusions. The Hindu appears at least to deny the world, while the Zen Buddhist affirms it. So it is possible for the drug movement to go either way: toward a total rejection of the world or a total commitment to the world. To help clarify the alternatives, we shall explore the conclusions of Zen and related concepts in some detail. To provide still another option, we shall look into the evolutionary-theological theories of Teilhard de Chardin, applying them to the questions raised by LSD and Asian metaphysics.

In sum, it is the argument of this book that a relationship exists between LSD cultism and radical theology; that both offer a legitimate challenge to orthodox theology; that both reflect an introduction into the West of Eastern religious ideas; that LSD may provide the basis for a humanistic ethics; that contemporary currents indicate a renewed interest in metaphysics in general, ontology in particular; that there is some evidence of a nascent revolt against science and rationalism; that all of these developments carry with them both dangers and promises. If the church is challenged, it has been challenged before. If men have lost their God before, they have always managed, somehow, to find him again. If legitimate questions are raised, there also are legitimate answers to those questions, and we shall suggest what some of them might be.

The drug movement has been characterized as a weak-kneed retreat from reality. In reply, the cultists assert that the truth is just the other way around: it is we who flee reality and they who accept it. They alone have faced the dreadful knowledge that comes when one encounters the Clear Light of the Void. Only they have dared to turn and see what makes those flickering shadows on the wall of the cave. Possibly the only way to settle the question is to follow these explorers all the way and enter with them into the secret inner world they say they have discovered. And if you do that . . . well, they are not cowards. They are very brave, perhaps, or very wise, or very dull and foolish. Craven they are not.

2 Through psychedelic eyes

On a good trip the LSD voyager may feel he has penetrated to the godhead itself. But is it really the godhead he sees? Or is it the Medusa?

Before we describe what LSD does, let us first ask what it is. That is a much easier question to handle, admittedly, and it is mildly ironic that this is so. Where the mysteries of nature are concerned, the situation is usually reversed, as Bertrand Russell has pointed out in the case of electricity. Science can describe very accurately what electricity does but hasn't the foggiest notion what it really is. As for LSD, it is a synthetic drug: d-lysergic acid diethylamide tartrate, compounded from a constituent of a rye fungus known as ergot. Its general history by now is a twice-told tale and then some, so we shall be brief about it. LSD was first synthesized in 1938 by Dr. Albert Hofmann, a

26

biochemist at the Sandoz pharmaceutical firm in Basel, Switzerland; but the scientist did not know what he had created until 1943, when he accidentally inhaled or otherwise absorbed a small amount of LSD and thus discovered the drug's curious properties. It produced uncanny distortions of space and time and hallucinations that were weird beyond belief. It also produced a state of mind in which the objective world appeared to take on a new and different meaning. These effects, and the agents which produce them, are now referred to as psychedelic —a generic term which means "mind manifesting," which in turn means nothing. The word has come into common usage simply because of its neutral connotation; due to the controversy involved, it is the only word so far that all sides have been willing to accept. It is used as both noun and adjective.

Unlike heroin, opium, and alcohol, LSD apparently is not addictive. This means simply that prolonged use of the drug, so far as we can tell at this time, does not create a *physiological* craving or dependency based on changes in a subject's body chemistry—changes that are produced by liquor and junk— and there are no physiological withdrawal symptoms when use of the drug is terminated. LSD on the other hand may be *psychologically habituating;* but this, after all, can also be said of chewing gum and television.

There are literally scores of psychedelic substances, natural and synthetic, and LSD is only one of many agents capable of producing a full-fledged psychedelic experience. Identical effects can be obtained from Indian hemp and its derivatives, including hashish; from the peyote cactus and its extract, mescaline; from a Mexican mushroom and its laboratory counterpart, psilocybin, which Dr. Hofmann synthesized in 1958. Hemp and peyote have been used as psychedelics for centuries, and mescaline was on the market before the turn of the century. LSD's uniqueness lies in the fact that it is very easy to make— and mega-potent. According to the Food and Drug Administration, a single gram of LSD can provide up to ten thousand doses, each of them capable of producing an experience lasting up to twelve hours or longer.

Scientists seized upon the drug as a tool for research and therapy, and literally thousands of technical papers have been devoted to it. Since LSD appeared to mimic some symptoms of psychosis, it offered possible insights into the sufferings of mental patients—although psychotherapists later came to doubt that it produces what was first referred to as a model psychosis. Preliminary research indicated it might be useful in the treatment of alcoholism and neurosis, and it also served to ease the anguish of terminal patients. In small doses, in controlled situations, it appeared to enhance creativity and productivity. But the public at large knew nothing of LSD until 1963, when two professors, Timothy Leary and Richard Alpert, lost their posts at Harvard University in the wake of charges that they had involved students in reckless experiments with the drug. Leary went on to become more or less the titular leader of the drug movement, in which capacity he soon ran afoul of the law, and the movement spread to campuses and cities across the country. By and large, it seemed at first to develop as a middle-class phenomenon, attracting to its ranks mainly students and intellectuals, liberal ministers, artists and professional people, as well as bearded pariahs. Official panic provoked a wave of legislation which ended or seriously hindered almost all legitimate research programs; the legislation did little or nothing to discourage the drug movement, which received its supplies from black market sources.

Depending upon the point of view, Dr. Hofmann assumed the role of a Prometheus or Pandora. In correspondence I once asked him if he sometimes felt like the latter, to which he replied: ["In my opinion, every discovery in the field of natural science is to be positively viewed, and thus also the discovery of LSD. If one wishes to deplore the discovery of LSD, then one must also view the discovery of morphine negatively, for morphine, one of the most valuable gifts of pharmacy, is just as dangerous and destructive as LSD when used improperly. There are no forces in the universe that are bad in themselves. It is always up to man whether he will make good or bad use of them." And if Dr. Hofmann's words have a familiar ring, perhaps they are reminiscent of the statements nuclear physicists were making in 1945.

LSD is a colorless, odorless, tasteless drug. It is taken orally for the most part, and the precise nature of its action upon the brain and nervous system has not been determined. It is believed, however, that only a minute portion of the tiny dose ever reaches the brain, and even this disappears in less than an hour. Possibly, then, LSD sets off a reaction which continues long after the drug itself has been dissipated. As Dr. Sidney Cohen, a leading medical authority on LSD, expressed it, "The drug acts to trigger a chain of metabolic processes which then proceed to exert an effect for many hours afterward." In hipsters' terminology, the subject is "turned on." And the experience begins.

The nature of the experience will depend on countless factors, which are commonly summed up as "set" and "setting": that is, the mood of the subject and the environment in which the drug is administered. The subject becomes highly suggestible, and the slightest false note can result in the nightmare of a bad trip. Most experiences will include a hallucinatory period, in which fantastic visions occur, and in some cases it is possible to see sounds and hear colors—the result of sensory short-circuiting, referred to in the literature as synesthesia. One subject reported that he could taste the categorical imperative (which he said was something like veal). These very weird effects have received considerable publicity; when they are pleasurable, they—and sometimes sexual stimulation—constitute what may be regarded as the "kicks" aspect of LSD. But the drug movement cultists are not concerned with kicks in this sense. Skilled travelers say they can avoid the hallucinatory period altogether and thus are able to achieve and prolong the "central experience." There does appear to be such an experience, and this is what the cultists refer to when they speak of a good trip. It does not always occur, and some people may never achieve it; it must be sought after, perhaps, and expectation may be a significant factor in its production. But it does exist, and it is the very basis of the cult.

From various sources, then, let us see if we can construct a typology of this central or core experience. While the problems of description are notorious, in most cases the mind will appear to operate at a new level of consciousness in which:

1. The sense of self or personal ego is utterly lost. Awareness of individual identity evaporates. "I" and "me" are no more. Subject-object relationships dissolve, and the world no longer ends at one's fingertips: the world is simply an extension of the body, or the mind. The world shimmers, as if it were charged with a high-voltage current, and the subject feels he could melt into walls, trees, other persons. It is not that the world lacks substance; it is real, but one is somehow conterminous with it. And it is fluid, shifting. One is keenly aware of the atomic substructure of reality; he can feel the spinning motion of the

electrons in what he used to call his body, and he senses the incredible emptiness that lies within the atoms, where the electron planets circle their proton suns at distances which are comparably as vast as those in the solar system itself. Thus it seems only natural that one could pass through a wall, if only it were possible to get all the atoms lined up properly for just one moment. In the vastness of outer space, is it not a fact that billion-starred galaxies are able to drift through each other like clouds of smoke or astral ghosts, without the single collision of one star with another?

As for identity, it is not really lost. On the contrary, it is found; it is expanded to include all that is seen and all that is not seen. What occurs is simply depersonalization. The subject looks back on his pre-drug existence as some sort of game or make-believe in which, for some reason, he had felt called upon to assume the reduced identity or smaller self called "I." Being had concentrated its attention at a single point in order to create, and play, the game of writer, banker, cat burglar. Or so it now seems. If there is any analogy to this in normal existence, is it not perhaps the moment when one awakens from sleep? In that case, what is the first thing one asks oneself? "Where am I?" Or isn't it rather, "Who am I?" And then, in an effort of will, attention is concentrated to re-create the role that was lost in sleep. Thus in the drug experience, as in sleep, the normal state of tension is relaxed. Home at last, after that dreadful party, Being slips out of her stays, so to speak, and breathes an ontological sigh of celestial relief. Consciousness is allowed to scatter, and the subject at last can be Himself again.

The subject is somehow united with the Ground of his Being, with the life force that has created the visible world. He *remembers*. And what he remembers is the true identity that underlies all the individual egos of the world. He is one again with the universe, the eternal, the Absolute.

He has found himself again. He is made whole again. That which he once knew, he has remembered.

(But when did he know it? And when did he forget?)

2. Time stops. Or, in any case, it ceases to be important. And perhaps it would be more accurate to say that memory and forethought stop. The subject is content to exist in the moment— in the here and now. And time has no meaning in the here and now. Bergson suggested that the sense of time consists simply of arrests of our attention. Seconds and minutes do not really exist; they are artificially created "immobilities" dreamed up by science, which is unable to comprehend flux, mobility, or the dynamic character of life itself. Installed within true movement, said Bergson, the mind would lose its normal sense of time, since the normal function of the intellect is to foresee, so as to act upon things. "We must strive to see in order to see," he said, "and no longer to see in order to act." This is precisely what happens in the psychedelic experience, where forethought is anesthetized. Without forethought there is no anticipation. Without anticipation there is no desire. And time stops.

3. Words lose all meaning. In the here and now there are no abstractions. An object represents only that which it is. It is perceived as a *Ding-an-Sich,* a thing-in-itself, and it matters not whether Kant said that sort of perception is impossible. Kant never took LSD. If he had, he would have known that rose is a rose is a rose is a rose.

The same feeling is captured in childhood perhaps. As Wordsworth wrote, recalling his boyish days when nature was all in all:

> . . . I cannot paint
> What then I was. The sounding cataract
> Haunted me like a passion: the tall rock,
> The mountain, and the deep and gloomy wood,
> Their colours and their forms, were then to me
> An appetite; a feeling and a love,
> That had no need of a remoter charm,
> By thought supplied, nor any interest
> Unborrowed from the eye. — That time is past,
> And all its aching joys are now no more,
> And all its dizzy raptures.

The psychedelic experience is similar but multiplied at least a thousand times over. Coincidentally, Havelock Ellis wrote, after experimenting with mescaline in the 1890's: "If it should ever chance that the consumption of mescal becomes a habit, the favorite poet of the mescal drinker will certainly be Wordsworth."

But thing-in-itself perception is beyond all language. It is, in fact, the antithesis of language, which is the real cause of our normal inability to see the thing-in-itself. This is so because we think in words, and words are abstractions or symbols of things; as a result, we tend to think and perceive in symbols. Thus the American flag fluttering on the Fourth of July is seen in terms of Concord and Lexington. The flag-in-itself is never seen; we must always associate it with something else. And so on. And the English language is especially crippling because of its painful stress on simile and metaphor. Thus a rose isn't a rose; it's what my love is like. Ruskin quite properly attacked the pathetic fallacy as evidence of a "morbid state of mind." But the psychedelic experience suggests that all figures of speech reflect the same unhealthy attitude—and that speech itself is a web of deceit. The Greek poets sensed this. For the Greeks, as Edith Hamilton pointed out, a thing of beauty was never a symbol of something else, but only itself. A star was just a star, a primrose a primrose. "That a skylark was like a glow-worm golden in a dell of dew, or like a poet hidden in the light of thought, would have been straight nonsense to them. A skylark was just a skylark. Birds were birds and nothing else, but how beautiful a thing was a bird, 'that flies over the foam of the wave with careless heart, sea-purple bird of spring.'" And if symbols as such are deceptive, how much worse are the symbols of use. We look at a peach, and we see something to eat. We look at a field, and we wonder how many bushels of wheat it will yield. We meet somebody for the first time, and we ask ourselves what this new person can do for us. Can we play bridge with him? Sell him some insurance? Worst of all, we look at our loved ones even in terms of our own needs, emotional and otherwise. In the terminology of Martin Buber, we live in the world of I-It. We associate things, and we use things, and we never look at the thing-in-itself in the here and now. Moreover, we cannot look upon an object without thinking the word which symbolizes it. Tree. Lamp. Table. But the psychedelic world is the world of pure experience and pure relation; it is the world of I-Thou. In this world, for example, a tree is not a source of timber or shade. A tree is to look at. And it is not a tree. It is *that*, there. Now. And that is a that is a that is a that.

4. There are no dualities. Sweet and sour, good and evil—these also are abstractions, inventions of the verbal mind, and they have no place in the ultimate reality of here and now. As a result, the world is just as it should be. It is perfect, beautiful.

It is the same world that is seen without LSD, but it is seen in a different way. It is transfigured, and it requires no meaning beyond the astonishing fact of its own existence.

What does "meaning" mean anyhow?

Meaning is just one more abstraction, implying some future use or purpose; it has no place in the here and now of naked existence. And is this perhaps the significance of the Eden story? They ate of the tree in the midst of the garden, and their eyes were opened, and they became as gods, knowing good and evil. The first dualism, fundamental to all others. What does this story represent if not the introduction into the world of a new way of thinking and a new form of perception? What does it refer to if not the evolutionary product we describe so proudly as intellect, or the rational mind? What does it signify if not that moment when man looked about him and said for the first time: "This is wrong." Not, "This hurts me," or "The tiger is chewing my leg, and I wish he wouldn't." No. "This is *wrong.*" What an idea! What a curious concept. No doubt it was the greatest, or worst, idea that man ever had. It marks that point in the process of becoming when life took charge of itself. Man had accepted the world; now he decided to judge it. Thus Adam became the first existentialist, taking upon himself the nauseating responsibility that turned Sartre's stomach. In doing so he laid the basis for those existential anxieties which are nothing more or less than ontological anxieties. He estranged himself from his environment; worse yet, he alienated himself from the very Ground of his Being. In Eden he had lived in perfect I-Thou relation, neither judging things nor subsuming them with words. East of Eden lay the world of I-It, where the ground was cursed for his sake, and the Lord told him what he could expect from it. Thorns and thistles he could expect from it.

35

So Adam was cast out of the garden, his own mind the flaming sword that would prevent his return. He lived in the world of I-It, and he sought there for meaning. But he never found it, and none of those who came after him have found it.

Men are frustrated in the search by their I-It minds of use, which have made meaning synonymous with purpose. Nothing is meaningful unless it leads to something else, or produces some future effect. Thus a man smokes *to* enjoy himself— and that is a meaningless action. But he puts on his shoes *so* he can go to the store—and that by definition is meaningful. But it is not meaningful enough, and man craves for an ultimate meaning. He wants his life to lead to something else, somewhere in the future. It doesn't, apparently, so he feels the anxiety of meaninglessness. Taking hope, however, he diagnoses his anxiety as a form of psychic pain. The sense of meaninglessness is meaningful in itself, he decides; it implies there is a meaning somewhere, and he is estranged from it. Which is so. But the ultimate meaning he seeks is in fact the absence of meaning—in the sense of purpose. Meaning is simple existence in the here and now. And of course man already lives in the here and now. The trouble is, he doesn't know how to live in it. And this is what LSD seems to tell him. It tells him that he is still in Eden, if only he knew it. It is only necessary to spit out the apple and look at the world through psychedelic eyes. The apple is his intellect, or way of looking at things, and under LSD his intellect no longer functions. Forethought is put to sleep, and he opens his eyes upon Paradise regained.

A voice whispers in his ear. It tells him: *"Essence precedes existence."*

5. The subject feels he knows, essentially, everything there is to know. He knows ultimate truth. And what's more, he

knows that he knows it. Yet this sense of authority cannot be verbalized (any more than the experience as a whole can be verbalized) because the experience *is* a whole which cannot be divided, and it transcends all partial abstractions. What is known is pure Being, which cannot be compared with anything else. The subject is identical with that which he knows and therefore is speechless. In any case, language can never describe that which language itself is responsible for negating. Finally, there is the problem raised by H. G. Wells in his tale of "The Richest Man in Bogota." To a race of eyeless men, how do you explain sight? What words do you use?

This describes the psychedelic experience, produced by a chemical. But it also describes something else.

It describes religious mysticism.

It describes the experience of saints and prophets since the first tick of history's clock. And it describes as well those flashes of insight that sometimes come to humbler folk in moments of prayer, or of grace.

3 Chemistry and mysticism

In its broadest sense, mysticism refers to direct communion with the divine; to intuitive knowledge of ultimate truth; to the soul's sense of union with the absolute reality that is the Ground, or the source, of its Being. And apparently it is impossible to distinguish this experience from the central experience produced by LSD and other psychedelic agents.

The classic accounts of mystical experience read like psychedelic Baedekers. In recent years, moreover, a number of studies have compared the two experiences, and the results have reinforced the idea that the experiences are in some way connected. The best known of these studies was undertaken by psychiatrist Walter Pahnke at Harvard University, where psilocybin was administered in a religious setting to ten theology students. Nine of the ten felt they had genuine religious experiences, and Pahnke concluded that the phenomena they reported were "indistinguishable from, if not identical with," a typology based on W. T. Stace's widely known summary of mystical experience.

At Princeton, students were shown accounts of a religious experience and a psychedelic experience, and two-thirds of the students identified the drug-induced experience as the religious one. In a book in which they summarize five separate studies, including Pahnke's, R. E. L. Masters and Jean Houston stated that "religious-type" experiences were reported by 32 to 75 per cent of subjects who received psychedelics in "supportive" settings, and by 75 to 90 per cent of those who received them in settings that included religious stimuli. And so on. The consensus of research seems to be that the two experiences are at least phenomenologically the same. This is a way of saying: "Well, they certainly *look* the same, and beyond that I'm not going to stick my neck out." What this neatly avoids, of course, is the problem of comparing the *sources* of the experiences.

Significant parallels to psychedelic experience are to be found in William James's observations on religious conversion, the faith-state, and mystical experience. Conversion occurs, said James, when a formerly divided self becomes unified, and "a not infrequent consequence of the change operated in the subject is a transfiguration of the face of nature in his eyes. A new heaven seems to shine upon a new earth." James made the point that "self-surrender has been and always must be regarded as the vital turning-point of the religious life." And the total abnegation of self or ego is without question the hallmark of psychedelic experience. "Only when I become as nothing," wrote James, "can God enter in and no difference between his life and mine remain outstanding." Discussing the faith-state,

James observed that it too is characterized by an objective change in the appearance of the world, which takes on a sweet and beautiful newness. "It was dead and is alive again. It is like the difference between looking on a person without love, or upon the same person with love." In addition, there is a loss of all worry: "the sense that all is ultimately well with one" and a "willingness to be." Finally, there is "the sense of perceiving truths not known before," and these "more or less unutterable in words." As for mysticism, James found that it also is marked by an ineffability requiring direct experience, as well as a noetic quality which carries with it "a curious sense of authority for aftertime." Still another aspect is passivity, in which "the mystic feels as if he were grasped and held by a superior power." And a final factor is transiency. "Mystical states cannot be sustained for long. Except in rare instances, half an hour, or at most an hour or two, seems to be the limit."

One of those rare exceptions perhaps was Emanuel Swedenborg, the so-called Swedish Aristotle, who was said to have had a mystical experience which lasted, more or less continuously, for almost three decades. LSD cannot match that record, but it does seem to improve somewhat on the normal time limits indicated by James. Except for duration, however, there is obviously a remarkable similarity between James's typology and psychedelic experience. And just incidentally, James noted that mystical states are often accompanied by various photisms, or luminous phenomena, which also are an aspect of psychedelic experience (for example, Paul's blinding vision and Constantine's cross in the sky). Finally, let us call attention to James's observation: "One may say truly, I think, that personal religious experience has its roots and centre in mystical states of consciousness." In other words, we are likening psychedelic experience not just to mysticism but to religious experience as a whole.

From this background, then, emerges LSD's first clear challenge to orthodox theology.

Did the saints owe their visions to some biological short-circuit which caused them to experience spontaneously what LSD cultists achieve with a chemical? Can their mystic raptures be traced to a malfunction of the adrenal glands? Does the faith-state have a neurological basis? Is the religious experience as such nothing more than a fluke of body chemistry?

The materialists would like to think so, and do. Dr. Sidney Cohen (who is no materialist) has suggested that religious experience may one day be redefined as "a dys-synchrony of the reticular formation of the brain."

Some scholars have pushed even further. Not only do psychedelics appear to duplicate religious experience, they say. It is possible that religion itself is psychedelic in origin. One of the major spokesmen for this viewpoint has been Gordon Wasson, an authority on the psychedelic mushrooms of Mexico, who has suggested that primitive men may have stumbled many times upon innocent-looking plants which produce the same effects as LSD. These theobotanicals, possibly mushrooms, might well have been a "mighty springboard" which first put the idea of God into men's heads. Wasson also has proposed a psychedelic explanation of the ancient Greek cult that produced the Eleusinian Mysteries, and he has advanced the idea that Plato's pure Ideas might be the product of a psychedelic insight. (In other words, Plato was an acidhead.) Following this line of reasoning, it might seem logical to conclude that the Eden story is actually a psychedelic parable—and we would be happy to propose that theory ourselves had we not already proposed another theory with an antithetical conclusion. In any case, Wasson goes on to suggest that psychedelic sacraments in the course of time may have been replaced by more innocuous hosts, and that they represent perhaps "the original element in all the Holy Suppers of the world." The whole idea, of course, is pure speculation, and necessarily so, but at the same time it is very interesting speculation and by no means implausible. It is particularly tempting to apply Wasson's theory to the metaphysics of India; according to Masters and Houston, an estimated 90 per cent of the holy men in that country are currently on hemp and various other drugs.

The point often is made that religious ascetics traditionally have promoted their mystical states of consciousness by employing techniques that rival LSD in their probable impact on biochemical balance. These include fasting, yogic breathing exercises, sleep deprivation, dervish dances, self-flagellation, and monastic isolation. Even in the pews of the pious, religious contemplation may be supported by such trance-inducing aids as organ music, stained glass windows, repetitive chants and prayers, incense, and flickering candles.

The question of religious chemistry has been underscored recently by the wide attention given to the theories, already mentioned, of Dr. Abram Hoffer and Humphry Osmond. Their adrenochrome-adrenolutin hypothesis suggests that schizophrenia may be caused at least in part by defective adrenal metabolism. Very briefly, the adrenal gland secretes the hormone adrenaline, which helps coordinate biological mechanisms in emergency situations—for example, a fist fight or a threatened traffic accident. Heart rate is increased, the blood is sugared up and pumped to the necessary muscles. Adrenaline also may affect the emotions, contributing to anxiety and depression. In the body it turns into a toxic hormone called adrenochrome, which in turn can be converted into either of two other compounds: dihydroxyindole or adrenolutin. It is possible that dihydroxyindole balances off adrenaline to reduce tension and irritability; in schizophrenics, however, adrenochrome is converted primarily into adrenolutin, which also is toxic, and the combination of adrenochrome-adrenolutin results in a poisonous disruption of the brain's chemical processes. That is the theory. And the prescribed antidotes are nicotinic acid (niacin) or nicotinamide (Vitamin B-3). Discussing one of the villains in the piece, the scientists write: "There are few who doubt that adrenochrome is active in animals or in man, and it is now included among the family of compounds known as hallucinogens—compounds like mescaline and LSD-25 capable of producing psychological changes in man."

The Hoffer-Osmond studies are far from conclusive, and similar theories have been advanced in the past. But the studies hold promise, and they are receiving serious consideration—due in part, no doubt, to the significance they have in other areas of current debate, including religion. The line dividing insanity and mysticism has never been too sharply drawn, and the biochemical theory of schizophrenia makes it all the more tenuous. Vitamin B-3 actually has cured cases of schizophrenia, according to Dr. Hoffer and Osmond. But Vitamin B-3 also has proved effective in terminating LSD experiences, and the implications of this must be obvious. As we asked earlier: Are insanity, mysticism, and the psychedelic experience in some way related?

Aldous Huxley has suggested they are. The experience of

absolute reality is awesome enough in small doses, and the schizophrenic, drugged by his own body chemistry, is like a man who is permanently under the influence of a psychedelic. He is "unable to shut off the experience of a reality which he is not holy enough to live with." He cannot take refuge, even for a moment, in "the homemade universe of common sense—the strictly human world of useful notions, shared symbols and socially acceptable conventions." The result is a bad trip which never ends. But the psychedelic subject knows that he can and will return to that limited but comforting world, and he is therefore in a position to accept his experience: to enjoy it and to learn from it. This in fact appears to be the main basis for denying that psychedelics produce a model psychosis. As Dr. Cohen and parapsychologist Gardner Murphy expressed it: "When the dissolution of the reasoning self occurs in a chaotic manner, the result is called psychosis. When the state is not accompanied by panic or anxiety, it is perceived as mystical, and creative solutions of (or at least an armistice with) life problems could result." Dr. Cohen has proposed that the difference here makes logical a distinction between insanity and unsanity, which he would place at polar ends of a continuum; in the middle, somewhere, would lie sanity. Nevertheless, it is a bit jarring to consider the possibility that religious experience is an end-product of adrenochrome, described as a dark crystalline material which can easily be made in a laboratory. "In its pure form," write Dr. Hoffer and Osmond, "it manifests itself as beautiful, sharp, needle-like crystals which have a brilliant sheen. When the crystals are powdered, it appears as a bright red powder, which dissolves quickly in water to form a blood-red solution."

It would be interesting to see if a shot of vitamins could terminate a spontaneous religious experience. But what if it did? And what if LSD does in fact initiate such an experience? Does this mean the experience is simply a manifestation of the drug?

4 The sound of one hand clapping

A spark touches off an explosion. But the explosion is not simply a product or property of the spark. If one opens a window and looks at the view, one does not equate the view with the window; one does not suppose that the window *caused* the view. In the same sense, LSD has been described as a chemical key which opens some window in the mind.

Similarly, electric shock may awaken a mental patient to the "reality" of the common-sense world, but nobody will say that the common-sense world is a product of the shock. By the same token, it could be argued that LSD awakens normal men to a still greater reality—and that it does so by means of a chemical shock which liberates the mind from ingrained thought patterns based on verbal abstractions and the memory-forethought habit.

Our normal mode of thinking can be described as survival-thinking. We see a traffic signal, and we think "stop" rather than "pretty red light." Furthermore, since our mind is designed to act upon things, we normally limit our perception to those things we wish to act upon. This is known as attention, a form of consciousness in which awareness is brought to a sharp but limited focus; we see what we have to see, and we see it the way we need to see it. Both abstraction ("stop") and attention are designed for action, and so we view the world in terms of our action upon it. Along these same lines, Huxley described the brain and nervous system as a "reducing valve" which receives the flood of sensory input and filters out all that which is not necessary for action, and therefore for survival; were it not for this, we could not function in the world as we know it. To function, we must deceive ourselves as to the actual nature of reality—a form of adaptation which LSD researcher Willis W. Harman has termed cultural hypnosis. "We are all hypnotized from infancy," wrote Harman, who went on to propose that this was just another way in which to describe enculturation. We accept suggestions from the environment—from our parents and society—and these suggestions shape the manner of our perception; finally, we perceive things in a state of hypnosis: not as they are, but as we are told to see them. Thus the child first sees the traffic signal as a pretty red light, which it is; but soon he learns to see it another way—as an abstraction—or else is run down by a truck. And so it must be.

Genius, however, has been defined as looking at things in just a slightly different way. Perhaps the truth of the matter is that genius looks at things more as they actually are: the genius is not completely hypnotized but only partly so. Reality is still reality, after all, and it does no harm perhaps to steal an occasional glance at it, if only to satisfy ourselves that it still exists.

LSD presumably allows us to do this by breaking the trance; it enables us, in Huxley's term, to become Mind at Large. The reducing valve is shut down, attention is scattered, and we are back again in the real world—happy and helpless. Comparing survival awareness and psychedelic awareness, Orientalist Alan W. Watts has suggested the analogy of a spotlight and a floodlight, and the analogy may be an apt one; it is true that the psychedelic subject often will focus his attention for long periods upon some object of delight—a flower, perhaps, or a crack in a wall—but as Watts put it, this is an unprogrammed mode of attention in which one looks *at* things rather than *for* things: the world is not chopped into pieces for purposes of action or cause-and-effect analysis. In any case, LSD from this point of view is simply a trance-breaking snap of the fingers— and the same applies to any chemical agent which might be involved in ordinary religious experience. The chemical does not determine the experience, it merely permits it. In this connection, we may read a certain significance into one of the LSD cultist's familiar expressions, "turned on." We turn on a radio and hear an orchestra playing *Vienna Bonbons,* and of course the music was there in the room all the time, and the music would be there even if the radio were not; the radio simply allows us to hear the music. The comparison is all the more valid if, as indicated earlier, LSD in fact does quit the brain after triggering its chain of metabolic processes, and it may be significant in this connection that some cultists say they have learned to turn on without drugs. And finally there is an interesting piece of evidence that has come to us all the way from Japan.

To produce the sudden insight called *satori*, many Zen Buddhists in Japan contemplate a "mind-murdering" form of riddle

48

called the *koan*. (What is the sound of one hand clapping? What was your original face before you were born?) These riddles of course defy logic, and that is just what they are supposed to do; they are designed to break down the rational intellect, just as LSD does, and thus provide the student with a new viewpoint. If asked to explain ultimate reality, a Zen master might kick a ball—or slap his pupil in the face. And the idea is that ultimate reality has nothing to do with words or logic: it is raw existence in the here and now. *Satori* is in fact remarkably similar to psychedelic experience, if not indeed identical, and it is produced by a form of shock which is neither chemical nor electrical but intellectual—or at least mental.

Still, the non-physical explanations of psychedelic experience raise many questions. If psychedelics simply awaken a subject to reality, why does the subject invariably return to his trance-state after a predictable interval? Why will another chemical terminate an experience? And what of psychosomatic medicine? Doesn't it suggest the possibility at least that Zen Buddhists and self-starting cultists have developed a capacity to influence their metabolism: that they somehow initiate a biochemical reaction which in turn initiates their experience? The issue of chemistry cannot be avoided, it seems; psychedelic cultists and religionists alike should be prepared to face squarely the possibility or even probability that their metaphysical systems are in fact inexorably linked to biochemistry.

This is not a new question; it is one of those very old questions we referred to earlier. And it revolves around the musty dispute between the materialists, who say that the soul or psyche is just an aspect or property of the material body, nothing more, and the dualistic idealists, who make a clear distinction between spirit on the one hand and matter on the other. According to the idealists, the soul merely inhabits the body, and it survives the body after death.

William James met the problem head on more than six decades ago in *The Varieties of Religious Experience*. He wrote sardonically: "Medical materialism finishes up Saint Paul by calling his vision on the road to Damascus a discharging lesion of the occipital cortex, he being an epileptic."

James himself had participated in experiments with nitrous oxide (laughing gas). This turn-of-the-century psychedelic produced what James referred to as the anesthetic revelation, and far from convincing him that religion was mere chemistry, it indicated to James that there were unfathomed realms of consciousness which "forbid a premature closing of our accounts with reality." James scoffed at "superficial medical talk" about hypnoid states, and he asserted that medical materialism was "altogether illogical and inconsistent."

Why?

If *all* states of mind are caused by some organic condition, then one "could as easily argue that the liver determines the dicta of the sturdy atheist as decisively as it does those of the Methodist."

The sturdy atheist has yet to answer that, but what about the Methodist? With its obvious capacity to alter states of consciousness, LSD might appear to make hash of dualistic idealism. Even if it does, however, materialism is by no means the only option that remains. An alternative can be found within orthodox tradition, and this is the alternative offered by Thomas Aquinas. One hesitates to speak for a saint, but it does seem entirely likely that Saint Thomas would have no trouble reconciling religious conviction with LSD or the adrenochrome-adrenolutin hypothesis.

Dualistic idealism derives from Plato and has been passed on to us by Saint Augustine and Descartes, among others. But Thomistic philosophy rejects it and proposes instead the unitary idealism of Aristotle. This affirms the reality of both the spiritual and the material, but it does not insist that they be viewed antagonistically—or indeed as separate entities. One might as easily distinguish the warmth of the sun from the sun. Mendelssohn's *Violin Concerto in E Minor* is no less beautiful because it issues from catgut and horsehair. One does not say, "It's merely catgut" or "It's simply horsehair." Nor does one listen to Fischer-Dieskau singing Schubert and say, "It's nothing more than epiglottis, after all." In the same sense, the human personality implied for Saint Thomas a combination of mind and matter, body and soul. He acknowledged a physiological factor in dreams, moods, insanity. He did believe that a certain spiritual element survives after bodily death; but he considered this soul without its body an insignificant phantom, and he held that human personality, as opposed to this phantom, is an indivisible union of spirit and matter. This view has serious implications for personal immortality, as we shall see later. But it also provides a framework for a religious interpretation of psychedelic phenomena.

The supposed necessity for religion to insist upon a soul-body dichotomy traces back to that original sin of the I-It mind, dualism. And it also reflects a primitive line of reasoning which Sir James Frazer described in *The Golden Bough*: "As the savage commonly explains the processes of inanimate nature by supposing that they are produced by living beings working in or behind the phenomena, so he explains the phenomena of life itself. If an animal lives and moves, it can only be, he thinks, because there is a little animal inside which moves it:

if a man lives and moves, it can only be because he has a little man or animal inside who moves him. The animal inside the animal, the man inside the man, is the soul."

Thus the Huron Indians supposed the soul had a head and body, arms and legs; for the Nootka the soul was a little fellow who stood erect inside the head, and whenever he fell over, you lost your senses; for many primitives the soul was a manikin exactly resembling its possessor, and it was proper to speak of fat souls and thin souls, or long souls and short souls. The soul could escape through the natural openings of the body; the Marquesans therefore would hold the mouth and nose of a dying person, and the Wakelbura of Australia would stick hot coals in the ears of a corpse to allow themselves a running start before the dead man's ghost took after them. The soul also could escape in sleep and wander about, so the children of Transylvania were instructed to sleep with their mouths shut, and it was bad form to awaken anybody suddenly—or worse yet, to move the body of a sleeper. In Bombay it was tantamount to murder to alter the appearance of a sleeper, painting a man's face perhaps or adding mustaches to a slumbering woman. Such notions may well amuse us, but one might ask how they differ in essence from the basic assumption of dualistic idealism. That assumption has always been difficult to defend, and there is perhaps no compelling reason for us to defend it. The proposition that spirit *is* a property of matter has assumed importance only because the dualists have been so outspoken in their insistence that spirit is *not* a property of matter. Once you grant the former proposition, it loses all its force as an anti-religious argument. That chorus of "merely" and "simply" and "nothing more than" becomes about as meaningful as the "nevermore" which Poe's raven was trained to repeat. We do not even know, really, what matter actually *is,* and as far as Thomism is concerned, for example, LSD apparently does nothing to destroy the religious premise—as James defined it. If anything, it strengthens the premise. From this point of view, it matters not that mystical experience has a chemical aspect. To say that it is physical as well as psychical is to say nothing at all. "Of course it is," Saint Thomas might well reply. "And what of that?"

In fact, some theologians and scientists alike regard LSD as a kind of telescope with which to scan the deep-space regions of the spirit: a discovery which will enable man to gain a far greater understanding of his religious instinct. Now mysticism can be produced in the laboratory. It can be analyzed under experimental conditions with proper controls. And some have predicted this could lead to an eventual reconciliation of science and religion: to a science of religions if not a scientific religion or indeed a religious science.

That could be a bit optimistic, and it might appear to patronize religion. Considering their contrary viewpoints, it might be asked whether the rational is suited to study the instinctive any more than the instinctive is suited to study the rational. But perhaps there is some hope for an accommodation. As religions professor G. Ray Jordan, Jr., put it, there is a chance at least that intensive research with LSD "might do much to provide empirical proof of a primary beingness in some sense conscious which is the mystical or intuitive base and perhaps goal of man's religious aspirations and behavior." That goes directly to the heart of the matter: the possibility that there is such a thing as absolute Being (not to be confused, by the way, with *a* Being) and that this gives life its direction and purpose. Absolute Being in this sense means an ultimate nature, either realized or potential—as an oak tree has the ultimate nature of an oak tree (realized), and an acorn has the ultimate nature of an oak tree (potential). If it could be demonstrated that absolute Being exists in the universe, this would of course knock the existentialist props from Sartre's basic proposition. (Incidentally, it is interesting to note that Sartre once participated in a mescaline experiment under psychiatric supervision, and he did not like it at all, as Masters and Houston report the incident in their excellent study, *The Varieties of Psychedelic Experience.* When Simone de Beauvoir telephoned the hospital to ask how he was doing, Sartre told her unhappily he was fighting a losing battle with a devilfish.)

As for the common future of science and religion, there is another possibility, and it was suggested long ago in *The Golden Bough.* Sir James considered science a natural outgrowth of religion, and in fact he traced a line of development from magic to religion to science. As Sir James saw it, magic was actually a primitive form of science; it was based on the assumption that there were immutable laws to the universe and that man could control them. Thus magicians fearlessly ordered the gods about, threatening to kill them or bash their heads if they did not obey. But there was a fatal flaw to magic, and this lay "not in its general assumption of a sequence of events, determined by law, but in its total misconception of the nature of the particular laws." In the course of time the wiser magicians realized their spells were not working, and they concluded the gods must be running the show after all. Thus the Age of Magic became the Age of Religion; the magicians became priests, and they prayed to the gods they had sought to command. The point is that magic preceded religion "and that man essayed to bend nature to his wishes by the sheer force of spells and enchantments before he strove to coax and mollify a coy, capricious, or irascible deity by the soft insinuation of prayer and sacrifice." But then man discovered new laws, and these truly seemed to work; the priests became proud magicians again, and the Age of Religion became the Age of Science. Sir James thought this was well and good, as it should be. But he added:

"Yet the history of thought should warn us against concluding that because the scientific theory of the world is the best that has yet been formulated, it is necessarily complete and final. . . . In the last analysis magic, religion, and science are nothing but theories of thought; and as science has supplanted its predecessors, so it may hereafter be itself superseded by some more perfect hypothesis, perhaps by some totally different way of looking at the phenomena . . . of which we in this generation can form no idea."

Today's magicians have found perhaps that their spells do not work quite as they had hoped. Members of the drug movement in turn may find Sir James's words prophetic, suggesting that psychedelic insight can supersede both science and religion as we presently understand them. Certainly the cultists imagine that they have just the thing Sir James indicated might be necessary: a totally different way of looking at phenomena.

Curiously perhaps, scientists have seemed somewhat more receptive to the idea than have religionists. Among the latter, there are those who deny that psychedelics offer any insight into the actual nature of deity or cosmos.

5 The god of the East

Toward the middle of the last century the poet Charles Baudelaire became a member of the famed Club des Haschischins in Paris. He was initiated into the mysteries of hashish, one of the derivatives of psychedelic hemp, and he later wrote of the drug in something less than glowing terms. Baudelaire declared that the "accursed sweetmeat" resulted in "an appalling thing, the marriage of a man to himself." It led to "the individual's belief in his own god-head." In short, it made a man feel he *was* God.

A similar objection to the psychedelic experience was lodged more than a hundred years later by Professor R. C. Zaehner of Oxford, an authority on Eastern religions and a Roman Catholic. Zaehner set himself the task of replying to Huxley's enthusiastic claims for mescaline, and to play fair the professor took mescaline himself. "I disliked the experience," he reported, and what especially displeased him, as he put it, was the fact of losing control of oneself. "My conscious resistance to the drug was, indeed, very strong." That was not a very propitious set, as the cultists say, and as a consequence no doubt Zaehner's experience was limited to a sort of silly jag which often occurs in the early stages of a complete experience. Everything seemed utterly ridiculous and totally funny, and Zaehner laughed himself to tears. He described *The Golden Bough* as one of the great comic classics, and he said the trouble with Jung was "he doesn't realize how dull his collective unconscious is." Cultists believe this period of cosmic laughter reflects a first dawning of the awareness that words and normal perception patterns are both artificial and inadequate. In any case, Zaehner never went beyond it, and even in his most mirthful moments, he said, he managed to distinguish between funny and sacred objects. Shown a reproduction of a praying figure in a nativity scene by Piero della Francesca, he remarked that this was "a holy thing not to be looked at when you're drugged." Later he evaluated the experience as in a sense anti-religious—not conformable with religious experience or in the same category— and he reported with some pride that his normal religious consciousness "was never completely swamped." Zaehner's book, *Mysticism, Sacred and Profane,* is so far the most authoritative attack upon psychedelics from the viewpoint of orthodox religion, and in it the professor denies the idea that drugs might give rise to a genuine state of mystical consciousness. Zaehner concedes that psychedelics might promote what he terms natural mysticism and monistic mysticism, in which the subject feels a sense of union either with nature or with some impersonal Absolute; but they do not promote *Theistic mysticism,* in which the subject encounters the transcendent, personal God of Judaism and Christianity. That at least is Zaehner's opinion, to which he adds: "In the case of Huxley, as in that of the maniac, the personality seems to be dissipated into the objective world, while in the case of theistic mystics the human personality is wholly absorbed into the Deity, who is felt and experienced as being something totally distinct and other than the objective world."

In Theistic mysticism, Zaehner explains, the subject is conscious only of God and loses his awareness of all other things. In Huxley's brand of mysticism, one identifies himself with the external world—to the apparent exclusion of God.

From his own point of view, Zaehner may be right. But there is reason to dispute even his basic premise—that psychedelic drugs cannot promote Theistic mysticism—and his statements in any case are somewhat confusing if not confused. The Zaehner test for authenticity does not compare the psychedelic experience to mysticism as such. It compares it to Western mysticism. And that is just the point. There also is Eastern mysticism, which is older even than Western mysticism, and in fact it is just here that the drug movement offers its second major challenge to orthodox theology.

Zaehner to the contrary, Westerners under the influence of psychedelics very often have reported overwhelming awareness of a transcendent God; on the other hand, they also have reported the experience of alien concepts which frankly astonished—or even terrified—them, and these by and large have been the concepts of Eastern mysticism. Within the drug movement, moreover, it seems fair to say that the tendency has been toward the latter type of experience. There are subjective factors which may help to account for this tendency, and we shall discuss them later. But for the moment we can say that psyche-delic experience on the whole frequently appears to validate Eastern ideas about God, man, and the universe.

This of course is a very broad statement and possibly a very hazardous one; it assumes that it is possible to speak of Eastern ideas as such, as if these constituted a monolithic system of belief. The fact is otherwise, it scarcely needs to be said, and in one sense it is just as misleading to speak of Eastern religion as it is to speak of Western religion, thus bedding down together the Unitarian, the Roman Catholic, and the Seventh-day Adventist. It is not even proper to speak in general terms of Hinduism as such, or Buddhism as such, or even Hinyana Buddhism and Mahayana Buddhism as such. Each is a major system which contains various levels of sophistication and paths to the truth; in India, for example, you will find one Hindu worshiping a whole pantheon of Gods (330 million, according to one count, including the elephant-headed Gunputty), while another Hindu contemplates a metaphysical abstraction: you will find one Hindu who denies the world and another Hindu who is totally involved in the world. As you delve into Eastern thought you reach a level of interpretation which seems to correspond with at least some elements in Western thought; at a still deeper level it becomes almost impossible to say any-thing positive at all. But we shall call attention to some of these finer points, and meanwhile the fact remains that there is *some-thing* the Westerner refers to mentally when he uses that term, Eastern ideas. Perhaps in what follows it might be more cor-rect to say that we are describing Eastern ideas as they are generally viewed in the West, from a more or less superficial point of view, and that for the most part (in this chapter) we are describing the ideas of India rather than those of China or

Japan: that is to say, we are talking more about Hinduism than Buddhism, and a rather rudimentary Hinduism at that. Within such a context, then, riding roughshod over nuances, it might be said that psychedelic experience is Eastern in so far as it appears to validate immanence rather than transcendence, monism rather than pluralism, reincarnation rather than resurrection, nirvana rather than heaven, maya rather than hell, ignorance rather than evil, liberation rather than salvation, and self-knowledge rather than grace, redemption, or atonement.

As applied to the concept of God, transcendence refers to a form of deity whose nature is wholly different from man's. Theistic transcendence implies a wholly-other God who is some sort of supreme Person, in the sense at least that he can and does enter into a personal relationship with man. In strict transcendence, God and man are no more the same person than a master and his servant are the same person. In immanence, on the other hand, men partake of God's nature; God dwells in men, and they are in fact a part of God. The concept of immanence as such is perfectly acceptable from the viewpoint of Western Theism, so long as it does not deny altogether the element of transcendence. Thus it is fine to say that in God we live and move and have our being, in the orthodox interpretation of that phrase, just so we do not develop some fancy notion that we *are* him. The relationship in this case is crudely that of a father and son perhaps, as opposed to that of a master and his servant. But in pure immanence, or pantheism, God's nature and man's nature are identical. God is just another word for mankind as a whole, or the universe as a whole, or reality as a whole, or the life force as a whole. In pantheism it is neither insanity nor heresy to imagine you are God, because in fact you are God. Western theology on the whole has tended to emphasize the transcendent aspect of God—certainly so at least in comparison to Eastern theology, which has tended to emphasize the immanent aspect of God. In Asia, moreover, the emphasis has been given to pure immanence or pantheism, and God in any case is not conceived from a Theistic viewpoint as in any sense a person or being who dwells apart.

Consider next the doctrines of monism and pluralism. Pluralism insists upon the integrity of the individual soul, self, or ego. In monism, the individual personality has no lasting reality. It is a passing phenomenon, illusory in nature, and, in the end, all of the individual selves will be absorbed again into the godhead: into the One, the Whole, the Absolute, like drops of water in a termless sea. The godhead perhaps has temporarily divided itself for some practical purpose, as the hand is divided into five fingers; or more likely the godhead is simply amusing itself, making all the world a stage on which it acts out the various roles—a method of killing eternity, as it were. In Hinduism, this monistic Absolute is known variously as Atman or Brahman, and all individual selves are but aspects of Atman or the supreme Self. A Hindu holy man contemplates the sacred syllable OM, emblematic of the Atman godhead, and he asks, "What is that?" He is told, "Thou art that." Thus the wise Hindu is never jealous, for of whom should he be jealous? He sees no other, hears no other, knows no other, for what other is there to see, hear, or know? He hates no living creature—not even the tiger—for he knows that all creatures are simply food: are born from food, live upon food, and then become food. As the hissing Hamadryad in *Mary Poppins* put it: "It may be that to eat and be eaten are the same thing in the end. . . . Bird and beast and stone and star—we are all one, all one."

61

As cream in butter, as salt in the sea, Atman is in everything and is everything. Atman is like a flame which assumes the shape of each object it consumes. As the air in a jar is nevertheless the same as the air outside the jar, although it takes the shape of the jar, so the Self in every self is nevertheless Atman. And the wise Hindu knows this. He knows that he himself is the youth, the maiden, the old man bent upon his staff, the dark butterfly, the green parrot with red eyes, the thundercloud, seasons, and seas. Buddhists, in reverence, refuse to limit reality even to a universal Self, and thus they never speak of Atman. They speak instead of the Void or of the Clear Light of the Void. But the Void is not a void in the Western sense; the expression is a *via negativa* which seeks to avoid the trap of language, because there are no words—even Atman—to describe that which is beyond all words and beyond all determinations.

But call it Atman or call it the Void, enlightenment comes when the individual self realizes it has no separate identity beyond this Absolute. Such liberating awareness is referred to as *moksha* by Hindus and *satori* by Zen Buddhists, and with it comes that perfect peace in which the individual self achieves nirvana and is absorbed into the Absolute.

In the Theistic mysticism of the West, strictly speaking the soul is not absorbed by the Absolute, or by God. Rather, the soul and God retain their distinctive identities, and their relationship is one of love. Love is the key word that distinguishes Theistic mysticism from Eastern mysticism; it implies a relationship between two separate entities, and it therefore preserves both the transcendent nature of God and the everlasting integrity of the individual human soul. The soul is not sucked up by the Absolute as water is sucked up by a sponge; the soul relates to the godhead in an act of love, and the soul in fact may be referred to, in this relationship, as the Bride of Christ. As Buber expressed it in terms of his I-Thou relationship, I-Thou necessarily implies both an I and a Thou; I is not Thou and Thou is not I, but I and Thou are united in love: hence the significance of that hyphen.

In the Asian doctrine of absorption, of course, the achievement of nirvana can mean different things, depending upon the interpretation. It can mean an actual release from the world, physically and psychically, or simply a new state of consciousness in which one is no longer deceived by his intellect and therefore views the world as it actually is, beyond language and appearances. But nirvana commonly has been associated with the former interpretation, and this leads directly to the Asian concept of reincarnation—as opposed to resurrection. Resurrection was an Egyptian idea; it supposes that man has but one life upon the earth and thus only one chance to win his just and lasting reward, whatever that might be. On the judgment day of Western theology, the soul will be reunited with its body to find eternal life in a pluralistic heaven. Saint Thomas among others found it necessary to insist upon resurrection; with his rejection of dualistic idealism, it seemed the only way to provide for the personal immortality of the individual soul, and this point was the main basis for Thomas' famous quarrel with Averroism. Averroes had denied the possibility of personal immortality and had proposed instead the theory of monopsychism: the idea that mankind as a whole has a single mind in which all individuals participate. It is said that Thomas considered personal immortality the most important issue of the thirteenth century; he defended it vigorously, and Averroism was anathematized by the bishop of Paris in 1270.

But resurrection and the permanence of the individual soul also are denied by the East. In the alternative doctrine of reincarnation, the separate self does not really exist, and it is only the realization of this fact which permits the achievement of nirvana. But realization is difficult—far more difficult than good works or avoiding sin. So a man is given not one life in which to achieve it, but many lives. The soul passes from body to body in a cycle of death and rebirth, as a leech proceeds from one blade of grass to the next, and each life offers a fresh opportunity to make the great discovery in which one recognizes at last the nature of the Grand Illusion. With the discovery comes the death of the individual personality, which never was, and absorption into the monistic Absolute or the everlasting peace of nirvana. This doctrine also has been interpreted symbolically as a poetic expression of the many stages that one man passes through in one lifetime, just as nirvana has been interpreted to mean a state of awareness rather than literal absorption into nirvana which leaves the earth behind. But the goal in any case bears no similarity to the phenomenal heaven of the West. State of mind or state of Being, it is not a place, and the individual personality is not an aspect of it.

In the same sense, there is no Eastern equivalent to the Western hell. If there is a hell, it is the world itself, or at least the deceiving world of appearances—the phenomenal illusion which is known as maya or sangsara. A man lives in hell when he fails to recognize reality. He lives in hell when he denies his own true nature and is therefore tormented by lust and desire. It is his mistaken sense of individuality which causes all of his pleasure and all of his pain, and there is far more pain than pleasure. He is a victim of dualism, hopelessly enmeshed in *meum et tuum*. Because he imagines that there is an other, he envies or desires the other. Because he imagines that his little self is his real Self, he weeps at the thought of his own mortality —for he knows full well that the little self is finite and that one day it must perish forever. But with enlightenment comes peace, serenity, and release from this hell. The wise man knows that there is no other, so he does not envy or desire the other; he is free from craving. The wise man knows that there is no little self, so he does not weep for his own mortality; he knows that there is only Atman or the Void, there is only the One, and he is that One, and therefore he is in fact immortal and can never perish.

It also follows, from the Eastern viewpoint, that evil deeds are a product of ignorance. Evil in the Western sense is just one more example of dualistic perception. It suggests there is a very real, if negative, force which causes man to sin against the light. But ask the Western moralist what would happen if a potential murderer were somehow spirited away to a tropical island and left there alone. This would-be killer would have nobody to kill, and so of course he would not kill anybody. On judgment day, shall he be judged a murderer or not? The problem is easily resolved in the East, where all men in a manner of speaking are stranded upon that island. It is impossible to kill anybody else, because nowhere in the universe is there anybody else. There is no other, except as imagined. In doing harm to what he supposes is another person, therefore, a man does harm only to himself. Homicide is impossible; there can only be partial suicides. And so it is, according to the doctrine of maya, that men do wrong through ignorance. They sin against others, and thereby against themselves, because they are deluded as to their true nature—because they fail to understand that they and their fellows are but elements of a monistic whole. Thus knowledge is the path to righteousness, and he who has knowledge will never sin. Thus the goal of wisdom is liberation from maya.

It follows that Eastern liberation is not the same as Western salvation. The Westerner must work for his own salvation, but ultimately it comes to him only through the love and mercy of God. In an act of grace, the transcendent deity may bestow his gifts upon some erring soul. For Christians, man's redemption was secured by the sacrifice on the cross, a direct intervention of the supernatural power on behalf of mankind. But in the East there is no supernatural power to intervene. There is no forgiveness, for there is no God who is able to forgive. The burden of liberation falls entirely upon the individual, who must lift that burden himself; he cannot pray that it be lifted from him. He must strive for liberation through self-knowledge, and in doing so he is helped or hindered by his karma—the sum total of a man's thoughts and actions during his lifetime or his lifetimes. He will be helped if it is good karma, hindered if it is bad karma.

Bad karma might seem at first to correspond with Western guilt, but it does not really. Guilt implies that sinful action is provoked by the active powers of darkness—by the force called evil—and that free-willed man has perversely chosen darkness over light. A clear-cut choice and the freedom to choose are basic assumptions in the doctrine of guilt, and the whole idea is foreign to Eastern thinking. There may be a choice, but there is nothing clear-cut about it. It is obscured by maya, which prevents a man from seeing it. If he could see it, there is no question what his action would be; he would do the right thing without a moment's hesitation, because the right thing is simply the logical thing: it is the selfish, or if you will the Selfish,

course to follow. Bad karma arises from ignorance, not perver-
sity. It has been equated with cause-and-effect and with
heredity. One remains a prisoner in the Net of Illusion because
one has not been thinking the right thoughts—has not gained
the proper knowledge, in other words—and heredity is another
way of saying that karma follows you from one generation to
the next, or from one reincarnation to the next. Evangelists such
as Billy Graham have complained bitterly that people no longer
believe in guilt, and Saint Augustine in his time felt called upon
to condemn a similar trend. In the latter case, the false prophet
was the astrologer, who suggested that a man's faults lay in
his stars, while the tempter's voice today belongs to Freud. And
perhaps America at least is moving toward an Eastern view of
sin. It has been said that an American takes delight in his
analysis, talks about it freely, and has a penchant even to boast
about it, while a European is still ashamed of his libido and
would not dream of discussing it in public.

But the world as illusion does not sit very well with traditional American concepts, and some would view this idea as
a greater threat to our values than pantheism, monism, or any
of the other Eastern isms. It seems to assert that life itself is
a curse, and indeed the Hindu speaks of life as a terrible wheel
of death and rebirth; reincarnation in his eyes is a curse, and
a new birth is something to be avoided at any cost. This might
be taken as a direct challenge to the Christian doctrine that
being as being is good *(esse qua esse bonum est),* and, as mentioned, some elements within the drug movement seem to have
found it an attractive idea. Moreover, it could be argued that
modern physics supports the basic proposition with its formula
that energy equals mass times the velocity of light squared
$(E = MC^2)$—suggesting that matter after all is not the solid,

substantial stuff we had supposed it to be. Nor is this just another idea of some woolly-headed philosopher; it is an idea that blew up Hiroshima and Nagasaki.

These various ideas represent the religious tradition of half the world. Insofar as it confirms them, therefore, the psychedelic experience cannot be dismissed as non-religious on the grounds laid down by Zaehner and Baudelaire, who really meant that it is non-Western.

It seems fair to say, moreover, that most drug cultists *do* interpret the LSD experience as a confirmation of Eastern metaphysics.

Timothy Leary, the high priest of LSD, has often appeared a bit vague on this point in his public statements. While he expresses himself for the most part in Hindu and Buddhist terminology, he tends to speak of the experience simply as "religious" in nature—suggesting that the religions of the East and West are fundamentally the same. Shortly after he founded his League for Spiritual Discovery, however, I asked Leary if there are not in fact certain basic differences between the Eastern and Western views. He agreed that there certainly are. I then asked him whether he thought LSD experience supports the pantheistic Eastern God or the transcendent Western God. And he told me there is no question about it—the experience supports the Eastern God, not the Western.

Even so, is it necessary to regard Eastern thinking merely as threat and challenge? As we have already indicated, many of the Eastern concepts are subject to different levels of interpretation—and some of them at least, at certain levels, may be entirely compatible with Western trends of thought. Furthermore, we might demonstrate that these Eastern ideas are not so foreign to the West as they may seem.

6 The dome of many-colored glass

"The Malay has been a fearful enemy for months," Thomas De Quincey wrote in May 1818. *"I have been every night, through his means, transported into Asiatic scenes."*

The entry is contained in the famous drug addict's auto-biographical account, *Confessions of an English Opium Eater.* The passage which follows describes the Eastern nightmares produced by the Eastern drug, and it is worth quoting at length:

> I know not whether others share in my feelings on this point; but I have often thought that if I were compelled to forego England, and to live in China . . . I should go mad. The causes of my horror lie deep; and some of them must be common to others. Southern Asia, in general, is the seat of awful images and associations. As the cradle of the human race, it would alone have a dim and reverential

69

feeling connected with it. But there are other reasons. No man can pretend that the wild, barbarous, and capricious superstitions of Africa, or of savage tribes elsewhere, affect him in the way that he is affected by the ancient, monumental, cruel and elaborate religions of Indostan, etc. The mere antiquity of Asiatic things, of their institutions, histories, modes of faith, etc., is so impressive, that to me the vast age of the race and name overpowers the sense of youth in the individual. A young Chinese seems to me an antediluvian man renewed . . . nor can any man fail to be awed by the names of the Ganges, or the Euphrates. It contributes much to these feelings, that southern Asia is, and has been for thousands of years, the part of the earth most swarming with human life; the great *officina gentium*. Man is a weed in these regions. The vast empires also, into which the enormous population of Asia has always been cast, give a further sublimity to the feelings associated with all Oriental names or images. In China, over and above what it has in common with the rest of southern Asia, I am terrified by the modes of life, by the manners, and the barrier of utter abhorrence, and want of sympathy, placed between us by feelings deeper than I can analyze. I could sooner live with lunatics, or brute animals. All this, and much more than I can say, or have time to say, the reader must enter into, before he can comprehend the unimaginable horror which these dreams of Oriental imagery, and mythological tortures, impressed upon me. Under the connecting feeling of tropical heat and vertical sunlights, I brought together all creatures, birds, beasts, reptiles, all trees and plants, usages and appearances, that are found in all tropical regions, and assembled them together in China or Indostan. From kindred feelings, I soon brought Egypt and all her gods under the same law. I was stared at, hooted at, grinned at, chattered at, by monkeys, by paroquets, by cockatoos. I ran into pagodas: and was fixed, for centuries, at the summit, or in secret rooms. . . . I fled from the wrath of Brahma through all the forests of Asia. Vishnu hated me: Seeva laid wait for me. I came suddenly upon Isis and Osiris: I had done a deed, they said, which the ibis and crocodile trembled at. I was buried, for a thousand years, in stone coffins, with mummies and sphinxes, in narrow chambers at the heart of eternal pyramids. I was kissed, with cancerous kisses, by crocodiles; and laid, confounded with all unutterable slimy things, amongst reeds and Nilotic mud. I thus give the reader some slight abstraction of my Oriental dreams, which always filled me with such amazement at the monstrous scenery, that horror seemed absorbed, for a while, in sheer astonishment. Sooner or later came a reflux of feeling that swallowed up the astonishment, and left me, not so much in terror, as in hatred and abomination of what I saw. Over every form, and threat, and punishment, and dim sightless incarceration, brooded a sense of eternity and infinity that drove me into an oppression as of madness. . . . [And] many times the very same dream was broken up in the very same way: I heard gentle voices speaking to me . . . and instantly I awoke: it was broad noon; and my children were standing, hand in hand, at my bedside; come to show me their colored shoes, or new frocks, or to let me see them dressed for going out. I protest that so awful was the transition from the damned crocodile, and the other unutterable monsters and abortions of my dreams,

71

to the sight of innocent *human* natures and of infancy, that, in the mighty and sudden revulsion of mind, I wept, and could not forbear it, as I kissed their faces.

De Quincey's attitude might well reflect English provincialism at its best, or worst, but surely he was correct in assuming that some of the causes of his horror are shared by others. Undoubtedly he has summed up very well the reaction of the average Westerner to that nebulous something we have referred to as Eastern ideas. A similar attitude was expressed, for example, by Grecophile Edith Hamilton in her comparison of Greek and Eastern art. The Greeks, she wrote, were the first Westerners, introducing into the ancient world something completely new: the rule of reason and the supremacy of the rational intellect. The Greeks loved order, they loved life, and they embraced with joy the beauty of the visible world. They were the first people to play, and their games were conducted on a grand scale. But this point of view was unique; it did not belong "to the immense expanse and the multitudinous populations of the East." With its oppressed masses and its wretched conditions of life, the East was preoccupied with the unseen—and with death. So insecure and unbearable was the visible world that men could find hope only by rejecting outside fact and turning inward to the invisible world of spirit and intuition. Thus a tomb in Egypt and a theater in Greece. "The one comes to the mind as naturally as the other." Thus a grotesquely stylized Hindu bronze of Shiva, its many arms and hands curving outward—and the Olympic Hermes, "a perfectly beautiful human being, no more, no less."

When Egypt ended, the East went on ever farther in the direction Egypt had pointed. The miseries of Asia are a fearful page in history. Her people found strength to endure by denying any meaning and any importance to what they could not escape. The Egyptian world where dead men walked and slept and feasted was transmuted into what had always been implicit in its symbolism, the world of the spirit. In India, for centuries the leader of thought to the East, ages long since, the world of the reason and the world of the spirit were divorced and the universe handed over to the latter. . . . The mystical artist always sees patterns. The symbol, never quite real, tends to be expressed less and less realistically, and as the reality becomes abstracted the pattern comes forward. The wings on Blake's angels do not look like real wings, nor are they there because wings belong to angels. They have been flattened, stylized, to provide a curving pointed frame, the setting required by the pattern of the composition. In Hindoo art and its branches, stylization reaches its height. Human figures are stylized far beyond the point of becoming a type; they too are made into patterns, schematic designs of the human body, an abstraction of humanity. In the case of an Eastern rug all desire to express any semblance of reality has gone. Such a work of art is pure decoration. It is the expression of the artist's final withdrawal from the visible world, essentially his denial of the intellect. . . . Again, the gigantic temples of Egypt, those massive immensities of granite which look as if only the power that moves in the earthquake were mighty enough to bring them into existence, are something other than the creation of geometry balanced by beauty. The science and the spirit are there, but what is there most of all is force, inhuman force, calm but tremendous, overwhelming. It

reduces to nothingness all that belongs to man. He is annihilated. . . . The Greek temple [on the other hand] is
the perfect expression of the pure intellect illumined by the
spirit. No other great buildings anywhere approach its
simplicity. . . . Majestic but human, truly Greek. No super-
human force as in Egypt; no strange supernatural shapes
as in India; the Parthenon is the home of humanity at
ease, calm, ordered, sure of itself and the world. The
Greeks flung a challenge to nature in the fullness of their
joyous strength. They set their temples on the summit
of a hill overlooking the wide sea, outlined against the
circle of the sky. . . . To the Greek architect man was the
master of the world.

In so far as it remains Greek, and therefore rational, the Western mind no doubt abhors Oriental images and the metaphysical
concepts they might seem to imply. Indeed, many Occidentals
have emerged from a psychedelic experience with the same sense
of horror and relief De Quincey felt when he awakened from
his opium-haunted dreams to find himself safe again in merry,
common-sense England. As we have already suggested, however,
those images and concepts are not as remote as they may appear.
They are and always have been an aspect of Western tradition,
as counterpoint if nothing more, and it would probably be possible to demonstrate their influence in almost every phase of
Western history. We have no intention of doing so. The task
is beyond us and would serve no useful purpose here; without
any attempt at comprehensiveness, however, we shall try to
show how this or that thread of Eastern thought has appeared
from time to time in the Western fabric.

The earliest of the threads can be picked up in Greece itself.

It was Heraclitus who observed that no man can step twice into the same stream. The phenomenal universe is not the secure and dependable piece of real estate our senses suggest; on the contrary, it is in a constant state of flux and chaos. Nothing stays the same. The only thing that never changes, said Heraclitus, is the fact that everything is changing. Thus the visible world of the West was called into question from the very beginning, and philosophical attempts to refute Heraclitus led in turn to the hypothesis of an invisible realm beyond the senses. Parmenides, for example, proposed that reality consisted of pure Being: an eternal One, never changing, which had no describable qualities whatever, except for the fact that it existed—and since existence in this sense did *not* change, what then of that phenomal world where everything changed? Obviously, it did not really exist.

Then came Plato with his eternal Essences or Ideas, which Gordon Wasson has suggested were psychedelic in origin. "The eye and the ear and the other senses are full of deception," said Plato. The soul is a helpless prisoner of the body. It is "simply fastened and glued to the body." Or so it was until philosophy came to its rescue. Referring to the soul in the feminine gender, Plato said that philosophy advised her to abstain from all use of the senses "and be gathered up and collected into herself, bidding her trust in herself and her own pure apprehension of pure existence, and to mistrust whatever comes to her through other channels and is subject to variation; for such things are visible and tangible, but what she sees in her own nature is intelligible and invisible." The soul is "dragged by the body into the region of the changeable, and wanders and is confused; the world spins round her, and she is like a drunkard, when she touches change. . . . But when returning into herself she reflects, then she passes into the other world, the region of purity, and eternity, and immortality, and unchangeableness, which are her kindred, and with them she ever lives."

Platonism evolved into the Neo-Platonism expounded by Plotinus, who preached a doctrine of mystical union with the Absolute. Both Platonism and Neo-Platonism in turn were assimilated by Christianity, and in fact they provided the metaphysical roots of the early church. This was due largely to the enormous influence of Saint Augustine, who was a Neo-Platonist before he became a Christian. Plato's pure Ideas were interpreted to be the thoughts of God, and as such Platonic philosophy continued as the mainstay of Roman Catholicism until the rediscovery of Aristotle in the thirteenth century. Saint Thomas became the most articulate spokesman for this revived school of thought, arguing the case for intellect, reason, and the interdependence of the spiritual and the material. And so it was that Platonism gave way at last to Aristotelianism, mysticism to empiricism, and Augustinianism to Thomism. Thomism in essence was officially adopted by the Roman Catholic Church. But the break really was not all that sharp, even within the church, and Platonism has continued to be a major influence in Western theology and philosophy. Today's drug movement might even be described as a sort of Neo-Platonist revival.

The point is that Plato was talking Net of Illusion talk and that this so-called Eastern idea is entirely within the Western tradition—the idea that the phenomenal world does not really exist; or the idea that our truncated senses cannot perceive ultimate reality; or the idea that our intellect deceives us. Take Berkeley, take Hume. Take almost any Western philosopher you would care to name. Take modern physics, for that matter. It seems clear that the West mistrusts the visible world just as much as the East does, and always has. The only real issue has been, in James's terminology: Does some unseen order lie beyond that visible world, and should we seek to adjust thereto?

Platonism also contains other Oriental threads. Plato, too, spoke of a morality based wholly on knowledge. He spoke of reincarnation and of concepts equivalent to nirvana and karma. For example, Socrates in the *Phaedo* is discussing the fate of the soul after death:

> That soul, I say, herself invisible, departs to the invisible world—to the divine and immortal and rational: thither arriving, she is secure of bliss and is released from the error and folly of men, their fears and wild passions and all other human ills, and forever dwells, as they say of the initiated, in company with the gods. . . . But the soul which has been polluted, and is impure at the time of her departure, and is the companion and servant of the body always, and is in love with and fascinated by the body . . . do you suppose that such a soul will depart pure and unalloyed?

Such souls are held fast by the corporeal. They haunt sepulchres and tombs. They

> . . . wander about such places in payment of the penalty of their former evil way of life; and they continue to wander until through the craving after the corporeal which never leaves them they are imprisoned finally in another body. And they may be supposed to find their prisons in the same natures which they have had in their former lives. . . . men who have followed after gluttony, and wantonness, and drunkenness, and have had no

thought of avoiding them, would pass into asses and animals of that sort. . . . And those who have chosen the portion of injustice, and tyranny, and violence, will pass into wolves, or into hawks and kites.

If the Greeks worshipped Apollo, god of reason, they were devoted also to Dionysus, the wine-drunk god of instinct and mysticism. The cult of the Eleusinian Mysteries paid homage to Dionysus, and it is believed the Mysteries included a theory of reincarnation. The possibility that the cult utilized some sort of psychedelic host would appear to gain considerable support from a Plutarch fragment, quoted by Edith Hamilton, which is thought to describe the Eleusinian initiation rites: "When a man dies he is like those who are initiated into the Mysteries. Our whole life is a journey by tortuous ways without outlet. At the moment of quitting it come terrors, shuddering fear, amazement. Then a light that moves to meet you, pure meadows that receive you, songs and dances and holy apparitions." As we shall see later, this passage suggests a remarkable parallel between the Mysteries and the contemporary drug movement's esoteric interpretation of the *Tibetan Book of the Dead*.

Reincarnation also was entertained as a doctrine by some of those Gnostic sects that flourished during the first three centuries of Christianity. The sects were Platonist in that they took a very negative view of existence in the world of appearances, and they taught that release could be obtained through a secret *gnosis* or knowledge of the divine order. They also assumed Plato's concept of the Demiurge—an imperfect creator god who made the earth, as opposed to the supreme and perfect god who exists as pure Being. They made of the Demiurge an evil, fallen deity who was responsible for the creation of matter and hence for the curse of phenomenal existence, for the fall from pure Being, for the Net of Illusion. The sects were a curious hodge-podge of Christian dogma, magic, and Eastern metaphysics.

Christianity had to absorb Gnosticism, just as it had to absorb Neo-Platonism, and the early church was plagued in addition by a whole spectrum of Asian-flavored heresies: for example, the Albigenses, the Bogomiles, the Paulicians. These sects adulterated their Christianity with strong doses of Eastern idealism, including the concept of the Demiurge and a hatred of matter. Similarly, Judaism had come under the dualistic influence of Zoroastrianism during the Babylonian Captivity. The precise extent of the East's impact upon the development of Judaism and Christianity is impossible to measure at this point in history; indeed, there is an equally frustrated body of scholarship which has attempted to demonstrate a Western impact upon Eastern religions during some period in the misty past. But there clearly was some East-to-West metaphysical commerce, and this has led to some rather airy speculation that the Bible contains an esoteric teaching along Eastern lines. Much is made of the fact that Jesus spoke in parables, and it is suggested that these perhaps were Oriental abstractions presented in parabolic style for the benefit of his unsophisticated flock. The people were not ready for meat, so he fed them milk. "And with many such parables spoke he the word unto them [the multitudes], as they were able to hear it. But without a parable spoke he not to them: and when they were alone, he expounded all things to his disciples."

Hidden meaning is thus read into many preachments. "The kingdom of God cometh not with observation." (The senses are trapped in the Net of Illusion.) "Neither shall they say, Lo here! or, lo there? for, behold, the kingdom of God is within you." (You are God.) "Inasmuch as ye have done it unto one of the least of these my brethren, ye have done it unto me." (We are a monistic One.) "Love thy neighbor as thyself." (You and your neighbor are the same person.) "Who is my mother? and who are my brethren?" (We are all the same person.) "If any man will come after me, let him deny himself. . . . For whosoever will save his life shall lose it: and whosoever will lose his life for my sake shall find it." (You must obliterate the ego to recognize your true Self.) "God is able of these stones to raise up children unto Abraham." (God is immanent in matter.) "A good man out of the treasure of the heart bringeth forth good things: and an evil man out of the evil treasure bringeth forth evil things." (Karma.) And so on. Small wonder, then, that no man dared ask Jesus any question after he declared, "Thou art not far from the kingdom of God." And the "I AM THAT I AM" of the Old Testament is obviously a Zen statement of pure experience. If nothing else, such conjecture indicates that truly great thoughts are like the commerce clause of the U.S. Constitution: they can be interpreted to meet any need in any period.

The thread of pantheism can be picked up again in the monopsychism of Averroes, the Great Commentator who was largely responsible for reintroducing Aristotle to the Western world. His theories fell short of pure pantheism, perhaps, for they included a remote First Cause; but they were both Eastern and heretical in their monistic denial of personal immortality, and they had gained considerable popularity in thirteenth-century Europe before Saint Thomas managed to reclaim Aristotle for the faith. Pantheistic tendencies appeared in the medieval Jewish mysticism of the Cabala, and the latter movement did much to shape the thought of Spinoza in the seventeenth century. The philosophy of the Jewish Dutchman was wholly pantheistic, equating God with creative Nature and creative Nature with God. Spinoza also denied the possibility of personal immortality. He did, however, speak of the immortality of the mind in language which might well set psychedelic bells to ringing: "Nevertheless we feel and know by experience that we are eternal. . . . Although, therefore, we do not recollect that we existed before the body, we feel that our mind, in so far as it involves the essence of the body under the form of eternity, is eternal, and that this existence of the mind cannot be limited by time nor manifested through duration." (A hundred micrograms of LSD will make that statement perfectly intelligible.) For his intellectual pains, Spinoza was excommunicated by his temple in Amsterdam. But he had considerable influence on later philosophers, including Hegel. Hegel's system of absolute idealism proposed that the universe consists of a single absolute Mind or Spirit which is attempting to realize and comprehend its own nature through an evolutionary process. Hegel in turn influenced such disparate thinkers as Karl Marx, Teilhard de Chardin, and Thomas J. J. Altizer.

Some of the more fragile nuances of Eastern philosophy perhaps are best caught in poetry—and the poetry of the West abounds in Oriental themes or hints of them. We could quote countless examples but will limit ourselves to only a few, offering them in the hope they may serve to sharpen some of these ideas, and to show that the ideas as such have a definite place in Western literature as well as philosophy.

Shakespeare, to begin with, certainly lends himself to an esoteric interpretation. The Delphic injunction, Know Thyself, is echoed in Polonius' fatherly advice to Laertes: "This above all: to thine own self be true, and it must follow, as the night the day, thou canst not then be false to any man." That might easily be taken to reflect the Hindu idea that men abuse one another only through ignorance of their monistic continuity, and that knowledge of the true Self therefore will automatically result in a perfect morality. And Hamlet himself sums up that delusion of the rational intellect which gives rise to the dualistic concept of evil: "There is nothing either good or bad, but thinking makes it so." Shakespeare plainly is a commerce-clause bard *par excellence,* and nobody has described the Net of Illusion so well as his Prospero:

> Our revels now are ended. These our actors,
> As I foretold you, were all spirits and
> Are melted into air, into thin air;
> And, like the baseless fabric of this vision,
> The cloud-capped towers, the gorgeous palaces,
> The solemn temples, the great globe itself,
> Yea, all which it inherit, shall dissolve,
> And, like this insubstantial pageant faded,
> Leave not a rack behind. We are such stuff
> As dreams are made on, and our little life
> Is rounded with a sleep.

We must of course include John Donne: "No man is an island, entire of itself; every man is a piece of the continent, a part of the main; if a clod be washed away by the sea, Europe is the less, as well as if a promontory were, as well as if a manor of thy friends or of thine own were; any man's death diminishes me, because I am involved in mankind; and therefore never send to know for whom the bell tolls; it tolls for thee."

Blake's poetry can be taken as a whole. It rejects the rational intellect and its dualistic perceptions, and indeed it gives the Eden story an interpretation quite similar to that suggested in an earlier chapter:

> Serpent Reasonings us entice
> Of Good & Evil, Virtue & Vice. . . .
> Two Horn'd Reasoning, Cloven Fiction,
> In Doubt, which is Self contradiction,
> A dark Hermaphrodite We stood,
> Rational Truth, Root of Evil & Good.

Blake had his own term for the Net of Illusion: "the mind-forg'd manacles." He rejected the intellect, the phenomenal world, the God of Theism. He rejected everything but man's eternal spirit, and he looked back with longing to the Universal Brotherhood of Eden, to the Universal Man, to the "Immortal Man that cannot Die." Blake in fact was a Gnostic, and his *Prophetic Books* revive the concept of the Demiurge. His Urizen ("your reason"?) is that sinister deity who was responsible for the fall from pure Being and the world of appearances.

> Earth was not: nor globes of attraction;
> The will of the Immortal expanded
> Or contracted his all flexible senses;
> Death was not, but eternal life sprung.

Then came Urizen with his ten thousands of thunders, and a shadow of horror was risen in Eternity.

> The Eternal mind, bounded, began to roll
> Eddies of wrath ceaseless round & round,
> And the sulphureous foam, surging thick,
> Settled, a lake, bright & shining clear,

White as the snow on the mountains cold.
Forgetfulness, dumbness, necessity,
In chains of the mind locked up,
Like fetters of ice shrinking together,
Disorganiz'd, rent from Eternity . . .

That eternal life, the furnace of all creation, was the subject of Blake's best-known poem, which Alfred Kazin has aptly termed "a hymn to pure being."
Pure Being, from which sprang the Tyger.

In what distant deeps or skies
Burnt the fire of thine eyes?
On what wings dare he aspire?
What the hand dare seize the fire?

After Blake, as might be expected, the Romantic poets come to mind—and one of the best examples would naturally be Shelley, who abandoned rationalism and atheism to become a full-blown Platonic idealist. As for the Passing Parade of Phenomena, compare that fragile speech of Prospero's and Shelley's stark:

"My name is Ozymandias, king of kings:
Look on my works, ye Mighty, and despair!"
Nothing beside remains. Round the decay
Of that colossal wreck, boundless and bare
The lone and level sands stretch far away.

Just as our contemporary mystics are dismissed upon the grounds of biochemical imbalance, so too has the Romantic movement been supplied now with a medical interpretation. The poets did not know it, but the source of their inspiration was a bacillus, the mood of that period resulting from the prevalence of tuberculosis. Keats was a victim of the disease, although Shelley insisted the critics had done his friend in, and Shelley's Platonic philosophy finds full expression in his elegy to the dead poet:

> The One remains, the many change and pass;
> Heaven's light forever shines, Earth's shadows fly;
> Life, like a dome of many-coloured glass,
> Stains the white radiance of Eternity,
> Until Death tramples it to fragments.—Die,
> If thou wouldst be with that which thou dost seek!
> Follow where all is fled!—Rome's azure sky,
> Flowers, ruins, statues, music, words, are weak
> The glory they transfuse with fitting truth to speak.

Then to Wordsworth, poet of the mescal drinkers. His ode, "Intimations of Immortality from Recollections of Early Childhood," includes the provocative stanza:

> Our birth is but a sleep and a forgetting:
> The Soul that rises with us, our life's Star,
>   Hath had elsewhere its setting,
>   And cometh from afar:
>   Not in entire forgetfulness,
>   And not in utter nakedness,
> But trailing clouds of glory do we come
>   From God, who is our home:
> Heaven lies about us in our infancy!
> Shades of the prison-house begin to close
>   Upon the growing Boy,
> But He beholds the light, and whence it flows,

He sees it in his joy;
The Youth, who daily farther from the east
Must travel, still is Nature's Priest,
And by the vision splendid
Is on his way attended;
At length the Man perceives it die away,
And fade into the light of common day.

The poem as a whole might appear to support the doctrine of pre-existence or reincarnation—an implication which Wordsworth later admitted "has given pain to some good and pious persons." He protested he had not intended "to inculcate such a belief." The poem was concerned with "that dream-like vividness and splendour which invest objects of sight in childhood," and Wordsworth had cast about in his mind for some device to express that vision, deciding finally to picture it as "presumptive evidence of a prior state of existence." He explained further: "I took hold of the notion of pre-existence as having sufficient foundation in humanity for authorizing me to make for my purpose the best use of it I could as a poet."

The argument about this stanza, and about Wordsworth's intentions, is extremely significant. It offers us a key. And that key fits many locks.

It may give us access to the real issues and deeper meanings that are still half-hidden below the surface of Eastern philosophy, the drug movement, and radical theology.

Professor Arthur Beatty, a Wordsworth authority, suggested that the poet really meant to say: "It is *as if* our birth were but a sleep and a forgetting." And that is the key.

Consider, for example, a comment that Coleridge made about the poem:

But the ode was intended for such readers only as had been accustomed to watch the flux and reflux of their inmost nature, to venture at times into the twilight realms of consciousness, and to feel a deep interest in modes of inmost being, to which they know that the attributes of time and space are inapplicable and alien, but which yet can not be conveyed save in symbols of time and space. For such readers the sense is sufficiently plain, and they will be as little disposed to charge Mr. Wordsworth with believing the Platonic pre-existence *in the ordinary interpretation of the words,* as I am to believe that Plato himself ever meant or taught it.

The italics are ours. And the point is simply this: that poets are poets, and they express themselves in the language of poetry —saying *"is"* when they mean *"as if."* Prophets are poets as well, and so are the great philosophers. And all poets, of whatever kind, have found it necessary at times to express their ideas in terms of symbol; the tools of their trade are the simile, the metaphor, the poetic image, the myth. The Greeks indeed may have held themselves aloof from the formal figures of speech, but they could and did make ample use of myth. So, too, perhaps did Jesus, Buddha, and those faceless authors of the Hindu holy books and the Old Testament. They were poets all. And we can only guess how often their *"is"* really means *"as if."* One is tempted to ask, of course, why they couldn't just come out with it—say what they meant and so have done with it—and the question is fair enough. In some cases, however, the people in fact may not have been ready for meat. In some cases it may be that the poet himself only half-knew what he meant—knew what he felt, all right, but could not quite put his finger upon it. In some cases he may have said what he meant and meant what he said, failing himself to apprehend the deeper meaning. And finally: he knew what he felt, and he knew what it meant; but what he felt and what he knew could not be expressed in conventional language. Such language simply did not apply in those twilight realms of consciousness where the poet explored the modes of inmost Being.

This is not as fuzzy as it may sound. Many of the discoveries of modern physics cannot be expressed in conventional language either; the physicists have been forced to leave language behind altogether, resorting instead to a complex mathematical symbolism—a form of myth, if you will—which cannot be retranslated into words. Many popular books have been written for the general public on the theory of relativity, for example; the fact remains that you cannot really understand the theory unless you have the math. Or so at least the mathematicians tell us, and we are prepared to take their word for it, while we are by no means ready to take the mystics at their word for anything. But the relativity theory is no less valid because it is expressed symbolically, for in fact everything is expressed that way. Expression as such is by definition symbolic: only the thing-in-itself is something more than a symbol of itself. Language and math, therefore, are equally symbolic; they are simply different kinds of symbolism. In any case, it follows that Plato did not necessarily mean that people really return to life as wolves, hawks, and kites; Blake did not necessarily mean that there really exists a deity comparable to Urizen; and *"is"* does not necessarily mean *"is"* every time it occurs in the various Hindu, Buddhist, Christian, and Jewish scriptures. It may in many cases mean *"as if,"* and, when so interpreted, these various scriptures perhaps are closer in meaning than they appear.

Using the key provided us, a case could be made that contemporary developments in theology and psychedelic experience can be explained essentially in terms of two basic myths and the conflict between them: the myth of the Demiurge and the myth of Ulysses.

Let us leave no doubt as to our own meaning. As we interpret it, the Demiurge is a symbol of the rational mind—of the cerebral cortex, which separates man from the beasts and (it may be) from much else besides. As for the Ulysses myth, we take it to suggest the presence of an evolutionary purpose in the cosmos: that is to say, an inherent state of Being as yet unrealized.

We shall return to these concepts later. Meanwhile, turning from Wordsworth, we skip ahead a few decades and look across the ocean from Europe to America.

7 Yankee Hindoos

The Orient's first substantial impact upon America occurred in a rather indirect manner, in 1492. Or the actual date might be placed two centuries earlier: it could well be argued that America owes its discovery to the Great Khan Kublai, lord of the Tartars, for the hospitality he showed Marco Polo in the thirteenth century. Columbus of course discovered the new continent while searching for the fabulous Cathay about which Marco Polo had written—and there is some irony in the fact that Polo's book contains one of the earliest accounts of the psychedelic experience.

Passing through Persia, the Venetian merchant learned the history of the Old Man of the Mountain, who lived in a castle which concealed a magnificent hidden valley. The Old Man invited youths to the castle, drugged them with hashish, and had them carried into the Valley of Delights, where they were wined and dined and entertained by dainty damsels. After four or five days the youths were carried back into the castle and told they had been in the Moslem Paradise. The Old Man could send them there any time he wanted, he said, if they would carry out his wishes—which usually meant killing somebody. This band of happy cutthroats became known as "hashshashins," from which we have derived the word *assassin*.

The barbarian invasions and the fall of Rome had cut the old Silk Road into Hither Asia, and later the Crusades served to divert Europe's attention still further from the Orient. There had been virtually no contact whatever between East and West when Marco Polo arrived in Tartary with his father and uncle, and indeed the Polos were the first Westerners Kublai Khan had ever seen. The promise of a restored relationship was shattered when the Chinese overthrew the Tartars and slammed the door on foreigners; then the Turks spread across Central Asia, effectively padlocking the door—and just incidentally forcing Columbus to seek a sea route to Cathay. The English penetrated India by the late seventeenth century, following the Portuguese; but China kept all foreign devils out until the middle of the last century, and Japan was a *terra incognita* until Admiral Matthew Perry sailed into Tokyo Bay in 1853.

It is understandable, then, that America was a long time making its own discovery of the East. The young country's first real introduction to Asian philosophy was provided by the New England Transcendentalists, whose writings were often a bewildering blend of Unitarianism and Orientalism, of Yankee self-reliance and Hindu self-abnegation. The influence of Romantic idealism and German philosophy also was evident. Thus readers of *The Dial* in 1841 found themselves asking, with Frederic Henry Hedge:

Hath this world, without me wrought,
Other substance than my thought?
Lives it by my sense alone,
Or by essence of its own?

Margaret Fuller wrote of Man as a whole: "As this whole
has one soul and one body, any injury or obstruction to a part,
or to the meanest member, affects the whole. Man can never
be perfectly happy or virtuous till all men are so."
Thoreau wrote of his inspiration:

I hear beyond the range of sound,
    I see beyond the range of sight,
New earths and skies and seas around,
    And in my day the sun doth pale his light. . . .

It speaks with such authority,
    With so serene and lofty tone,
That idle Time runs gadding by,
    And leaves me with Eternity alone. . . .

Such fragrance round my couch it makes,
    More rich than are Arabian drugs,
That my soul scents its life and wakes
    The body up beneath its perfumed rugs.

As the last stanza suggests, Thoreau undoubtedly would have
no part of LSD were he alive today. In *Walden* he observed, "I
prefer the natural sky to an opium-eater's heaven." The point
is, however, that Thoreau could turn himself on, needing only
that natural sky for a psychedelic, and he was wholly preoccupied
with the modes of inmost being. There was no object in going
around the world to count the cats in Zanzibar, he said. "Be

rather the Mungo Park, the Lewis and Clark and Frobisher, of your own streams and oceans. . . . Nay, be a Columbus to whole new continents and worlds within you, opening new channels, not of trade, but of thought. Every man is the lord of a realm beside which the earthly empire of the Czar is but a petty state, a hummock left by the ice. . . . it is easier to sail many thousand miles through cold and storm and cannibals, in a government ship, with five hundred men and boys to assist one, than it is to explore the private sea, the Atlantic and Pacific Ocean of one's being alone."

As for the dualism of good and evil: "I love to see that Nature is so rife with life that myriads can be afforded to be sacrificed and suffered to prey on one another. . . . The impression made on a wise man is that of universal innocence. Poison is not poisonous after all, nor are any wounds fatal." As for the verbal mind: "I know not the first letter of the alphabet. I have always been regretting that I was not as wise as the day I was born." As for the rational sense of time: "Time is but the stream I go a-fishing in. I drink at it; but while I drink I see the sandy bottom and detect how shallow it is. Its thin current slides away, but eternity remains. I would drink deeper; fish in the sky, whose bottom is pebbly with stars." And as for the comforts of formal religion: "I believe that men are generally still a little afraid of the dark, though the witches are all hung, and Christianity and candles have been introduced."

One passage in *Walden* strikes a particularly responsive chord for psychedelic cultists. Indeed, William James singled out the same passage as exemplifying those moments we all have "when the universal life seems to wrap us round with friendliness" and those hours "when the goodness and beauty of existence enfold us like a dry warm climate, or chime through us as if our inner ears were subtly ringing with the world's security." The oft-quoted passage:

> I have never felt lonesome, or in the least oppressed by a sense of solitude, but once, and that was a few weeks after I came to the woods, when, for an hour, I doubted if the near neighborhood of man was not essential to a serene and happy life. To be alone was something unpleasant. But I was at the same time conscious of a light insanity in my mood, and seemed to foresee my recovery. In the midst of a gentle rain while these thoughts prevailed, I was suddenly sensible of such sweet and beneficent society in Nature, in the very pattering of the drops, and in every sound and sight around my house, an infinite and un-accountable friendliness all at once like an atmosphere sustaining me, as made the fancied advantages of human neighborhood insignificant, and I have never thought of them since. Every little pine needle expanded and swelled with sympathy and befriended me. I was distinctly made aware of the presence of something kindred to me, even in scenes which we are accustomed to call wild and dreary, and also that the nearest of blood to me and humanest was not a person nor a villager, that I thought no place could ever be strange to me again. . . . "How vast and profound is the influence of the subtile powers of Heaven and of Earth! We seek to perceive them, and we do not see them; we seek to hear them, and we do not hear them; identified with the substance of things, they cannot be separated from them." . . . I only know myself as a human entity; the scene, so to speak, of thoughts and affections; and am sensible of a certain doubleness by which I can stand as

remote from myself as from another. However intense my experience, I am conscious of the presence and criticism of a part of me, which, as it were, is not a part of me, but spectator, sharing no experience, but taking note of it, and that is no more I than it is you. When the play, it may be the tragedy, of life is over, the spectator goes his way. It was a kind of fiction, a work of the imagination only, so far as he was concerned.

One wonders whether Huxley's antagonist R. C. Zaehner would dismiss that as natural mysticism or as monistic mysticism, or possibly as both. Theistic it is not.

Emerson probably did more than anybody else in his time to translate Eastern ideas, as he understood them, into the American idiom. He informed his readers about a school of thought, across the sea, which held that "what we call Nature, the external world, has no real existence—is only phenomenal. Youth, age, property, conditions, events, persons—self, even— are successive *maias* (deceptions) through which Vishnu mocks and instructs the soul." He added his opinion: "I think Hindoo books the best gymnastics for the mind, as showing treatment. All European libraries might almost be read without the swing of this gigantic arm being suspected. But these Orientals deal with worlds and pebbles freely." Emerson's poetry is freighted with Eastern imagery, and his "Brahma," for example, is almost a literal rendering of a passage from the *Katha Upanishad*:

> If the red slayer think he slays,
> Or if the slain think he is slain,
> They know not well the subtle ways
> I keep, and pass, and turn again.

For Yankee monists, Transcendentalism had this to offer:

> I am the owner of the sphere,
> Of the seven stars and the solar year,
> Of Caesar's hand and Plato's brain,
> Of Lord Christ's heart and Shakespeare's strain.

As with Blake, Walt Whitman's poetry as a whole seems to reflect the viewpoint of Eastern mysticism. In his later years Whitman gives the impression of somehow being in a permanent state of *satori,* and James indeed suggested that Whitman probably had "a chronic mystical perception." Rather tempting bait for speculation is offered by the fact that Whitman for so many years was little more than a journalistic hack. What was the source, then, of the inspiration which gave us *Leaves of Grass?* Following Wasson, it might be asserted that the Good Gray Poet at some period in his life was introduced to hashish or peyote or some other psychedelic, perhaps on that trip he made to New Orleans. The idea is farfetched, and we shall not pursue it; the fact remains that, spontaneously or otherwise, Whitman suddenly began to write poetry which echoes and re-echoes with Oriental and psychedelic intuitions:

> I celebrate myself, and sing myself,
> And what I assume you shall assume,
> For every atom belonging to me as good belongs to you.

Maybe it wasn't hashish; maybe it was Hegel. According to an 1882 entry in *Specimen Days,* the most profound theme to occupy the mind of man is the relation between the Me and the Not Me of the universe. And while Kant and Schelling perhaps had supplied us with partial answers, "G. F. Hegel's fuller statement of the matter probably remains the last best word that has been said upon it . . . illuminating the thought of the universe, and satisfying the mystery thereof to the human mind, with a more consoling scientific assurance than any yet." Long before that entry was made, however, Whitman had written in his journal of 1847: "I cannot understand the mystery, but I am always conscious of myself as two—as my soul and I." He was not contained between his hat and boots, he later wrote. There also was "the unseen soul of me." There also was the square deific, the One. There also was:

> Santa Spirita, breather, life,
> Beyond the light, lighter than light . . .
> Ethereal, pervading all, (for without me what were all? what were God?)
> Essence of forms, life of the real identities, permanent, positive, (namely the unseen.)
> Life of the great round world, the sun and stars, and of man,
> I, the general soul . . .

And just in case anybody should have missed his meaning:

> What do you suppose creation is?
> What do you suppose will satisfy the soul, except to walk free and own no superior?
> What do you suppose I would intimate to you in a hundred ways, but that man or woman is as good as God?
> And that there is no God any more divine than Yourself?
> And that that is what the oldest and newest myths finally mean?

For the general soul, read Brahman or pure Being; for Yourself, read Atman. Clearly, if Wordsworth speaks for the mescal drinkers, Whitman deserves consideration as the poet laureate of LSD. He also hinted at an esoteric doctrine of reincarnation, especially in "Crossing Brooklyn Ferry," and, like Thoreau and the three monkeys, he heard, saw, and spoke no evil. As we shall see, the innocent denial of evil in the universe is the basis for one of the principal charges that would later be lodged against Whitman, just as it is lodged now against the psychedelic drug movement.

America was given another injection of Eastern metaphysics in 1875, when the Theosophical Society was founded in New York City by Helena Petrovna Blavatsky and Henry Steele Olcott. Madame Blavatsky, a Russian, said that she had studied under an Eastern master in Tibet, and the Theosophists were effective in promoting many Hindu and Buddhist concepts including reincarnation, the monistic brotherhood of man, and the direct, mystical knowledge of a Universal Self. At the turn of the century, James's classic study of religious experience had a profound and lasting influence on theology and psychology; it opened the eyes of scholars and laymen to whole new realms of consciousness, probing deeply into the mystical awareness of East and West alike. On a lesser scale, R. M. Bucke helped to lay the groundwork for future developments by popularizing the concept of "cosmic consciousness." Bucke, a Canadian psychiatrist and a contemporary of James, wrote in 1901:

> The prime characteristic of cosmic consciousness is a consciousness of the cosmos, that is, of the life and order of the universe. Along with the consciousness of the cosmos

there occurs an intellectual enlightenment which alone would place the individual on a new plane of existence— would make him almost a member of a new species. To this is added a state of moral exaltation, an indescribable feeling of elevation, elation, and joyousness, and a quickening of the moral sense, which is fully as striking, and more important than is the enhanced intellectual power. With these come what may be called a sense of immortality, a consciousness of eternal life, not a conviction that he shall have this, but the consciousness that he has it already.

Bucke might easily have been describing the deep-seated conviction of a psychedelic cultist—and in fact some of the cultists have begun now to speak of themselves as a new species: as the forerunners of an emerging race of psychic mutants who will transcend the world to attain the nirvana of pure Being. Even at the time Bucke wrote, experimentation was beginning with various psychedelic agents then available. As mentioned, James himself was exploring the implications of nitrous oxide intoxication. Havelock Ellis had been dabbling with mescaline. And during the latter part of the nineteenth century, American Indian tribes had begun to use peyote as a sacrament in their religious ceremonies, leading finally to the establishment of the psychedelic Native American Church, which now has an estimated quarter-million members.

The new century saw a proliferation of cults, sects, and societies whose teachings often were a combination of mumbo jumbo and Eastern philosophy (for example, the I AM movement). Some of the issues at stake were translated to the secular and political level; the conflict between monism and pluralism reappeared in the antagonism between democratic individualism and the anthill conformity of fascism and communism: even the Rotary Club orator fulminating against creeping socialism and the Washington octopus was in a very real sense addressing himself to one of the most basic problems of metaphysics and East-West theology: the Many versus the One. As far as the laying of a groundwork is concerned, significance must also be attached to the new respectability which parapsychology gained as a result of the studies inaugurated at Duke University in 1930 by J. B. Rhine. The painstaking research devoted to such phenomena as extra-sensory perception and psychokinesis would lend its scientific aura to the astonishing statements which would later be made by the prophets of the drug movement, making those statements sound not quite so astonishing to an empirically minded generation. Indeed, it is possible that the Duke research has a direct bearing on the validity of psychedelic experience. As the ultra-cautious Rhine explained in 1947:

> The research in parapsychology even now touches other great issues of religion. If the mind of man is nonphysical, it is possible to formulate a hypothetical picture of a nonphysical system or world made up of all such minds existing in some sort of relationship to each other. This leads to speculative views of a kind of psychical oversoul, or reservoir, or continuum, or universe, having its own system of laws and properties and potentialities. One can conceive of this great total pattern as having a transcendent uniqueness over and above the nature of its parts that some might call its divinity.

Eastern themes were everywhere. Even the schoolgirl was

not immune as she turned the treasured pages of Kahlil Gibran's *The Prophet*. "Fare you well, people of Orphalese," said that chosen and beloved one, Almustafa. "A little while, and my longing shall gather dust and foam for another body. A little while, a moment of rest upon the wind, and another woman shall bear me."

The floodgates were opened by the outcome of the Second World War, of course, and one does well to remember that Zen was "camp" long before LSD. Buddhist study groups sprang up. American pupils and housewives could be found writing haiku poetry in grade-school classrooms and on the backs of grocery shopping lists. Bookstore racks gave prominent display to paperback editions of the *Upanishads,* the *Bhagavad-Gita,* the *Tao Tê Ching.*

These developments perhaps were inevitable; nevertheless, it seems fair to say that the Eastern influx could not have attained its present magnitude had it not been for the conscious and dedicated efforts of five men: Carl Jung, Daisetz T. Suzuki, Alan W. Watts, W. Y. Evans-Wentz, and Aldous Huxley. Jung's concept of the collective unconscious has Oriental connotations, and Jung in addition had an abiding interest in Eastern metaphysics: he lent the authority of his name to works on Zen and related subjects, writing forewords and commentaries which expressed his enthusiasm, and he once affirmed that the *Tibetan Book of the Dead* had been a "constant companion" to which he owed "not only many stimulating ideas and discoveries, but also many fundamental insights." Suzuki, a Japanese scholar who died only recently in Tokyo, wrote literally scores of books in which he sought to interpret Zen for Western readers, and he also lectured widely in American universities. Watts complemented Suzuki by examining Zen through Western eyes; a gifted interpreter and popularizer of complex ideas, he has made Eastern wisdom comprehensible to a vast audience through books, lectures, and television classes. Evans-Wentz introduced the West to the *Tibetan Book of the Dead,* a remarkable book which deserves our attention if only for the fact that it has since been adopted as the bible of the drug movement.

"It is a book which is sealed with the seven seals of silence," we are told in a foreword by Lama Anagarika Govinda. *"But the time has come to break the seals of silence . . ."* And why? Because "the human race has come to the juncture where it must decide whether to be content with the subjugation of the material world, or to strive after the conquest of the spiritual world." The origins of the book go back at least a thousand years. In the original Tibetan the work is known as the *Bardo Thödol,* which means "Liberation by Hearing on the After-Death Plane," and the exoteric purpose of the book was emancipation from the reincarnational wheel of death and rebirth. The book was read over the bodies of the recently deceased by those Sages of the Snowy Ranges, the Buddhist lamas of Tibet, and the idea was to talk a dead person out of seeking reincarnation in a new body. A dead man was believed to wander in the Bardo or After-Death Plane for forty-nine days (a symbolic number based on seven times seven), and during this period—in fact at the moment of death—he would encounter the Clear Light of the Void. If he had the understanding which comes with good karma, he would surrender his sense of individuality and would merge with that Void, thus ending the matter then and there. But the Void is terrible to behold if you lack understanding, and many reincarnations are normally required before one earns one's karmic passport to nirvana. And so it was that most dead men would turn in terror

from the Clear Light. They would wander in the Bardo, their senses assaulted by visions both frightful and beatific—by the Wrathful Deities and the Peaceful Deities—and finally they would enter the womb to be born again. In hopes of preventing this, the lamas would therefore read aloud from the sacred book, a sort of Fielding's guide to the Bardo region, and the dead men would thus receive detailed instructions for every stage of their journey. They would be told that their fear of the Clear Light resulted from their false sense of self, whose existence the Clear Light quite correctly appeared to threaten. They would be told that the visions they saw, apart from the Void, were nothing more than sangsara—projections of their own minds, which were still caught in the Net of Illusion. And finally they would be told that the womb was simply a doorway back to the world of appearances.

That was the exoteric teaching; but when Evans-Wentz first presented the book to the West, in 1927, the suggestion was made that it included or concealed an esoteric interpretation. Jung, for example, contributed a psychological commentary in which he asserted that "it is an undeniable fact that the whole book is created out of the archetypal contents of the unconscious." More to the point, Lama Govinda stated in his foreword that the book "was originally conceived to serve as a guide not only for the dying and the dead, but for the living as well." And that in any case is what it has since become, whatever the original intention might have been. More than a quarter-century after its initial publication, the Evans-Wentz edition came to prominence again in 1954, when Huxley made much of it in his very influential book, *The Doors of Perception*. In that book Huxley wrote of his first experience with mescaline, which he took in his home in California in the spring of 1953. Huxley reported that at one point he felt himself on the verge of panic, terrified by the prospect of ego disintegration, and he compared his dread with that of the Tibetan dead man who could not face the Clear Light, preferring rebirth and "the comforting darkness of selfhood." Thus the *Tibetan Book of the Dead* was inexorably linked to the psychedelic experience, and ten years later, in 1964, there appeared a volume titled *The Psychedelic Experience: A Manual Based on the Tibetan Book of the Dead.* The authors were LSD enthusiasts Timothy Leary, Ralph Metzner, and Richard Alpert, and they boldly offered their own interpretation of the ancient book: it had to do not with the death and rebirth of the *body* but rather with the death and rebirth of the *ego* in mystical states of mind. It was indeed a book for the living. More than that, it provided, in symbolic imagery, a precise account of the psychedelic experience. Absorption in the Clear Light is nothing more than a good trip, in which the psychedelic subject feels himself united again with the Ground of his Being. It is the apprehension of pure Being, beyond the sangsaric deceptions of language and rational perception. And those Peaceful and Wrathful Deities represent the hallucinatory period which occurs when one fails to achieve the central experience. A bad trip results inevitably when the subject refuses to face the Clear Light—violently resists the disintegration of his ego—and rather than seek rebirth in another body, he pleads for a shot of Thorazine which will return him to his own body in the phenomenal world of ego and rational symbolism.

Huxley's book has a certain historical significance; what we refer to today as the drug movement may be said to date from that book, although, as we have attempted to show, a substantial base for the movement had been in preparation long before

1954. In any case, the drug movement appeared to dovetail very neatly with what might be called the Eastern movement, and it might well be asked if this occurred naturally or under duress; that is, did the two really fit together, or were they made to fit? The latter possibility has been suggested by R. E. L. Masters and Jean Houston, who cite as evidence the phenomenon they refer to as "galloping agape." They assert that the supposed capacity of the psychedelics to promote feelings of brotherly love was rarely detected during early research in the 1950's: it became manifest only with the appearance of love-oriented drug literature. By the same token, Huxley and other drug enthusiasts are accused of leading their readers down the lotus path. Masters and Houston criticize the emergence of a "quasi-Eastern mystique," of a "wholesale leap to the East" and a "nebulous chaos seen as Eastern 'truth.' " These developments are all the more regrettable since the psychedelic drugs "may genuinely give some inkling of the complexity of Eastern consciousness."

Masters and Houston conclude: "To at least some extent the responsibility for this seduction of the innocent must lie with such authors as Huxley, Alan Watts, and others who in their various writings imposed upon the psychedelic experience essentially Eastern ideas and terminology which a great many persons then assumed to be the sole and accurate way of approaching and interpreting such experience."

The charge is serious, if it holds up in court. Does it?

8 The evidence of things not seen

Baudelaire complained in his time that ignorant persons thought of the hashish dream as a kind of magic theater where all sorts of miraculous things occur: wonders and marvels, all unexpected. But in fact, said the poet, hashish has no miracles to offer; all it does is exaggerate the natural, raising the same number to a higher power, and the hashish dream therefore will always be "the son of its father," reflecting the thoughts and impressions of the dreamer. Hashish is a mirror—"a magnifying mirror, it is true, but only a mirror"—and a man will see revealed in it "nothing except himself."

Evans-Wentz suggested that a wanderer on the Bardo plane would see the gods of his own pantheon: a Christian would see the Christian Heaven, a Moslem would see the Moslem Paradise, an American Indian would see the Happy Hunting

Ground, and a materialist would experience after-death visions "as negative and as empty and as deityless as any he ever dreamt while in the human body." The Tibetans taught, said Evans-Wentz, that the after-death state is indeed very much like the ordinary dream state, and whatever visions a man might see on the Bardo are "due entirely to his own mental-content."

There is no question that a subject under psychedelic influence is extremely vulnerable to suggestion, including auto-suggestion, and this might support the contention that the drug movement's Eastern orientation has been imposed upon it by an Eastern drug literature. One might also consider the fact that the drug experience historically has had Oriental connotations, for what could be a very prosaic reason. The hashish and opium of the nineteenth century came from the Orient, and the Eastern imagery which so haunted the European drug fiend might easily be explained as mental association. Even today the mere word "drug" may often serve to summon up visions of Fu Manchu and other sinister-looking Celestials.

The power-of-suggestion argument should not and cannot be lightly dismissed. What can be dismissed, however, is the contention that the psychedelic mystique is "quasi-Eastern" or "nebulous." Of course it *is* nebulous, as we suggested earlier, but that is neither here nor there; it is no more nebulous than any other metaphysical assertion which cannot be submitted to empirical demonstration. And it is not quasi-Eastern. It is Eastern.

If the problem was only one of imagery, suggestibility would no doubt be sufficient to account for it. There is no objective reason why LSD should evoke an image of a Chinese pagoda rather than a Western church, or Ishwara rather than Jehovah. As Evans-Wentz indicated, even the Eastern literature ac-

107

knowledges the subjective factor as far as visual content is concerned—and it can afford to do so precisely because it regards the Bardo visions as delusional: the phenomenal gods and paradises and hells do not really exist except in the mind of the dreamer, and that is just the point the Eastern philosopher is trying to make. It is only the Clear Light which matters and is real. Similarly, no particular importance is attached to the hallucinatory period in psychedelic sessions; all that matters is the central experience, which corresponds with the apprehension of the Clear Light. Nor is the terminology used of any significance. You can refer to the central experience as the Clear Light, or as God, or as anything you wish. The question which remains, then, is whether or not the central experience can be imposed by suggestion.

As for Baudelaire's statement, a drug cultist could easily turn it around to suit his own purposes. The psychedelics do indeed offer us a mirror, and a very accurate one at that. When a man looks into it, he sees nothing except himself—and this is just as it should be. That is the whole idea, right there. There is nothing else to be revealed.

We should keep in mind that the Eastern movement did not grow out of the drug movement; if anything, it was the other way around. The Eastern movement was well established when Dr. Hofmann made his serendipitous discovery, and the factors behind that leap to the East had little or nothing to do with suggestion. The Eastern movement absorbed the drug movement, and it did so because the central experience seemed to lend itself very well to an Eastern interpretation. But why weren't the Eastern implications obvious to begin with? Why did they have to be interpreted? Why didn't psychedelic subjects know they were having Eastern experiences? Why did they have to be told? A possible answer, of course, is that they did know—but did not know that they knew. They knew they were having some sort of an experience, but how were they to know it was an Eastern experience unless they had some knowledge of Eastern philosophy? If they did have the proper background, they might have recognized their experience as Eastern in nature—and certainly somebody must have done this at some point, or how else was the connection made in the first place? Huxley had a mescaline experience, and he decided it was Eastern; nobody had to tell him so: he told other people. But Huxley of course was Eastern-oriented; maybe it was auto-suggestion. And so the circle turns vicious.

Let us turn, then, to the people Huxley told, assuming they were not Eastern-oriented themselves, and let us ask why they believed him. They had an experience perhaps, and they did not know what to make of it; there was nothing they knew with which to compare it; they did not have the vocabulary to verbalize their intuitions or even to think them through; the concepts involved were new and startling, completely bewildering. Then Huxley and other Eastern enthusiasts provided a vocabulary and suggested various alternatives and possible conclusions which might be drawn from the experience. Somehow it seemed to fit, and people said, "Yes. That's it. That's exactly what it was." An analogy might be a robbery victim who flips through the photographs in a police rogues' gallery and then declares, "There, that's the man." Such victims unfortunately have been notoriously poor witnesses, and even their certainty leaves a reasonable doubt that a reliable identification has been made. Still, could a full-scale movement be generated by suggestion alone, with nothing substantial to support the suggestion? Surely there is something in the drug experience which makes the Eastern interpretation at least appear tenable. Furthermore, supporting evidence is provided by related developments in radical theology, where a leap to the East also is occurring, and without benefit of LSD. Watts and Huxley cannot be blamed for that.

Nor can they be blamed for the results of those turn-of-the-century experiments with nitrous oxide. Significantly, James found that the anesthetic (psychedelic) revelation tended to suggest "a monistic insight, in which the *other* in its various forms appears absorbed into the One."

Even so, from either point of view, we still are left with a Scotch verdict: not proven. And there the matter might rest, were it not for a final factor which has to do with mysticism as such.

The fact is that Western church authorities have generally regarded spontaneous mysticism with a measure of distrust and sometimes with open hostility. There is first of all the obvious objection that the mystic in a sense eliminates the middleman: he deals directly with God and thereby undermines the church's assumed right to act as religious arbiter. The second objection is less obvious but more important. It seems mysticism has shown a distressing tendency toward pantheism and monism, and the saintly mystic has often been a source of acute embarrassment to his church. We are talking now about Western mysticism. We are saying that Western mysticism has tended to be very much like Eastern mysticism; or, more accurately, all mysticism, Eastern and Western, has tended to be the same. James noted as a general trait of the mystic range of consciousness that it "is on the whole pantheistic and optimistic." He said further:

This overcoming of all the usual barriers between the individual and the Absolute is the great mystic achievement. In mystic states we become one with the Absolute and we become aware of our oneness. This is the everlasting and triumphant mystical tradition, hardly altered by differences of clime and creed. In Hinduism, in Neoplatonism, in Sufism, in Christian mysticism, in Whitmanism, we find the same recurring note, so that there is about mystical utterances an eternal unanimity which ought to make a critic stop and think . . .

Churchmen had stopped to think about it long before James made the suggestion, and they did not like what they were thinking. Mysticism too often had quite a lot to say about God's immanence and not very much to say about his transcendence; it had a lot to say about the divine encounter, but in many cases that seemed to imply a monistic absorption, not union through love.

Traditionally, the concern of the church has been in three areas: (1) the institutional, (2) the rational, and (3) the mystical. In the first, the church has sought to create a community of faithful with a heritage of common belief; in the second, it has sought to adduce logical proofs for the existence of God; in the third, it has sought to put church members in direct contact with the source of their faith. And every age has given these elements different emphasis.

Roman Catholicism has had its great mystic saints—Saint Theresa, Saint John of the Cross—but it also has had such thorns in the side as Master Eckhart, a Dominican, whose mystical utterances in fourteenth-century Germany sounded very much like pantheism. The rational Saint Thomas largely ignored mysticism, and Roman Catholicism took the position that God's existence could be proved intellectually. A severe reaction against mysticism occurred in the seventeenth and eighteenth centuries, led by the Jesuits and provoked in part by the excesses of the Quietists (Molinos, Madame Guyon, Fénelon). Quietism was accused of perverting the contemplative aspect of mystical experience; it recommended total annihilation of the mind, of the self, of all desire, including even the desire for salvation; it blurred or erased altogether the distinction between evil and good, man and God; wholly passive, it eschewed all thoughts and acts of service or devotion; it sought divine inspiration in the "soft and savory sleep of nothingness"; in its extreme form it produced a state of "mystic death" which bordered on catatonia. The practical and beloved Saint Theresa, reformer of the Carmelite Order, had combined the active and the contemplative life, as indeed had Jesus before her. By comparison, the Quietists appeared apathetic and amoral, if not immoral; they were charged with "idle basking in the divine presence," and their doctrines were condemned by Popes Innocent XI and Innocent XII. Mysticism in all its manifestations came under suspicion, and Catholics were advised that the mystical experience was a gift from God, not to be sought after. While this attitude was later softened, the Catholic reaction to Quietism quite likely has yet to run its course; nor can there be much doubt that the Vatican would tend to make a mental equation between the demand for a direct person-to-God relationship and the sort of thinking that resulted in the Reformation. Antagonism toward a mystical emphasis also was evident in Rome's dispute with the Catholic Modernists during the early years of the twentieth century. The Modernists could scarcely be accused of Quietism—they were in fact activists who believed in living their faith, and they strove for a liberal synthesis of the new science and orthodox belief. But they also were at odds with their church's stress on the rational knowledge of God, and especially so with the revival of the Scholastic tradition which was implicit in the emergence of Neo-Thomism. Rejecting religious intellectualism, they called instead for a religion of the inner way: of the heart, not the mind. Pope Pius X described their synthesis as a "synthesis of all heresies." Their doctrines were condemned in 1907, and the Modernist movement was crushed by excommunication.

We have already mentioned the mysticism of the Jewish Cabala, and in the following chapter we shall discuss at some length the flowering of Hasidism in the philosophical thought of Martin Buber. Turning to Protestantism, we find, as might be expected, that the mystic at first met with a friendly reception: the desire for a personal intimacy with God was one of the root causes of the Christian schism. Luther himself was a mystic. But even within Protestantism, restrictions were placed upon the complete freedom of intuitive experience—which led in turn to such developments as creedless Quakerism and the Quaker-meeting concept of personal communion with the indwelling Christ: the Inner Light. In the present century, Protestant mysticism came under fire from the heavy guns of Karl Barth and Emil Brunner. The barrage was devastating (or seemed to be), and, outside the revivalist's tent, spontaneous inner experience gave way to a general emphasis upon creeds and community of worship. Maybe it was not so much Barth as it was the overall decline in religious conviction—and therefore also in religious awe. Maybe it was just an end-product of secularization. But in any case it occurred. Or such at least was the opinion of Carl Jung and others who warned that the churches to their peril were ignoring their fundamental mission and their basic source of strength.

As the church critics saw it, that fundamental mission was to put men in personal touch with their God—to encourage, in other words, the divine-human encounter. And that basic source of strength was the mystical perception of the nonrational mind.

Such an argument makes mystical perception the primary source of religious faith. To follow the argument, however, it is necessary first to define faith.

A skeptic has defined faith as believing in something you know is not true. And many devout persons might actually agree with that. As Kierkegaard expressed the same idea, faith would not be faith if there were any rational basis for it. Faith and reason are mutually exclusive, the one beginning where the other ends, and a faith based on reason would be a contradiction in terms; it would in fact be reason, not faith: just one more example of ratiocination and logical analysis. Absolute faith recognizes the utter impossibility of its claim; to make the movement of absolute faith, you must first make the movement of absolute resignation—and then you believe anyway, "by virtue of the absurd." And this is faith. The knight of faith knows that "the only thing that can save him is the absurd, and this he grasps by faith." He acknowledges the impossibility, "and that very instant he believes the absurd; for, if without recognizing the impossibility with all the passion of his soul and with all his heart, he should wish to imagine that he has faith, he deceives himself." Paul Tillich expressed a similar view, insisting that absolute faith must be preceded by absolute doubt and despair. You confess that existence is meaningless, and then you accept your existence *in spite of* this—and this "courage to be" in the face of meaninglessness is in itself meaningful. Where does it come from, if not from Being itself? What does it represent, if not the power and the purpose of the godhead? "The act of accepting meaninglessness is in itself a meaningful act. It is an act of faith." And so on. But it is possible to define faith in an entirely different way as well, and perhaps an inkling of this can be found in *Hebrews:*

"Now faith is the substance of things hoped for, the evidence of things not seen."

John in his Epistle does not say that faith is based on the absurd; he says it is based on *evidence.* Science is based on the evidence of things seen. Faith is based on the evidence of things not seen. Both, then, are forms of deduction, and they differ only in the methods which they employ to gather their evidence: science relies upon the rational mind or the conscious; faith relies upon the intuitive mind or the unconscious. This is precisely what Jung was talking about: he said the churches were ignoring the vital role of the unconscious.

The churches perhaps were having enough trouble with science and so were in no mood to encourage a free-wheeling mysticism which might lead to a further erosion of orthodox dogma. But Jung and other critics believed that religion was making its stand on the weakest ground available. The logical proofs for God's existence were not very convincing. Even if they were, the intellect would reject them if instinct said no. Nor did it do any good to urge more faith, because faith is not an effort of will but, rather, a conviction based upon the evidence of things not seen. And the ultimate and only source of this evidence is the unconscious. "The unconscious," said Zen scholar Suzuki, "is the matrix of all metaphysical assertions,

115

of all mythology, of all philosophy." Years before, James had suggested that the unconscious was man's liaison to that unseen or mystical world for which the word God is "the natural appellation." He proposed that the unconscious sends us whispers of that other world "even as the waters of the infinite ocean send their waves to break among the pebbles that lie upon our shores." He said that all of man's ideal impulses appear to originate in that other world; if there *are* spiritual agencies out there, he argued, it seems only logical that they should communicate with us through "the subconscious continuation of our conscious life." "If there be higher powers able to impress us," he said, "they may get access to us only through the subliminal door." And Jung agreed. But he charged that the churches were concerned only with creeds—with "traditional and collective convictions which in the case of many of their adherents are no longer based on their own inner experience." Unreflecting belief, he said, "is notoriously apt to disappear as soon as one begins to think about it," and in any case it is "no adequate substitute for inner experience." The unconscious is "the only accessible source of religious experience." This does not mean the unconscious is God. It is, however, "the medium from which the religious experience seems to flow." It is not the role of the church, said Jung, to rope men into a social organization and reduce them to a condition of diminished responsibility. The care of the church should be the individual soul; the task of the church is "helping the individual to achieve a metanoia, or rebirth of the spirit."

From this point of view, the unconscious perhaps is comparable to a shortwave radio receiver. And the church has only one function: it should help men tune in on God's wavelength, so to speak, and after that it should drop out of the picture altogether, making no effort to interpret the transmissions—much less to jam them. The challenge to church authority becomes increasingly obvious, and indeed it has always been implicit not only in outright mysticism but in any form of devotion which emphasizes inner experience. The challenge was there long before the word "unconscious" was introduced to the vocabulary—the Tibetans meant the unconscious when they spoke of the Knower—and the German theologian Friedrich Schleiermacher as far back as 1799 was calling for a religion based exclusively on *Anschauung und Gefühl,* or intuition and emotion. A rejection of all creeds and dogma also was fundamental to the "spiritual Christianity" proposed four decades ago by the Russian philosopher Nicolas Berdyaev, and many other examples could be given. Huxley saw the urge for self-transcendence as "a principal appetite of the soul," and that appetite in our time has not been satisfied in church; today, "the sole religious experience is that state of uninhibited and belligerent euphoria which follows the ingestion of the third cocktail." Tillich pointed to the decline of religious awe: the question of our century perhaps was whether or not man could regain that sense of wonder he had once known in personal communion with the Ground of his Being.

Then came LSD.

With it has come a rebirth of awe. While some people might debate the assertion that this is religious awe, many members of the drug movement regard it as such—and the drug movement, as mentioned, has already produced a number of psychedelic churches, of which the Church of the Awakening may serve as an example. The church was incorporated in 1963 under the laws of New Mexico by John and Louisa Aiken, retired osteopaths. In a statement of purpose the church defines religion in its internal aspect as "the search within one's own consciousness for the Self, which is Being, which is Life." And to help the search along the church administers "the psychedelic sacrament." In a 1964 decision based on the First Amendment, the California Supreme Court ruled that Indian members of the Native American Church could not legally be deprived of the peyote used in their religious ceremonies. As a consequence of the widespread legislation against LSD, the Church of the Awakening and similar organizations such as the Neo-American Church and Timothy Leary's League for Spiritual Discovery have indicated they might seek a First Amendment court test to determine whether freedom of psychedelic religion applies also to the paleface, and the law's ultimate decision should prove to be of considerable interest, to say the least.

The drug cults make impressive claims. In the past, they say, religion probably had real depth for only a minority of churchgoers. Under the best of circumstances, a direct encounter with God was reserved for the special few; and even for them the experience was usually fleeting in nature. There are of course no statistics available on mystic percentiles, but it is just possible that psychologist Abraham H. Maslow offers us a rough clue with his concept of the "self-actualizing" person who is capable of achieving from time to time what Maslow has described as a "peak experience." We shall have much more to say about Maslow's psychology in a later chapter; for the moment, we are concerned only with his conclusion that self-actualization is possible for less than 1 per cent of the adult population. If peak experience and mystical experience are similar, and if Maslow's figure is reasonably accurate, it is rather interesting to find at the other end of the mental spectrum that schizophrenia is also said to affect about 1 per cent of the population. By comparison, the studies cited previously suggest that psychedelics can provide a mystical religious experience for up to 90 per cent of the population, which is certainly a considerable improvement. Now, say the cultists, with LSD it is possible for almost anybody to commune with God, any time he wants to, and for hours at a stretch. Now the common man can share the mystical visions of the saints themselves, and it is no longer necessary to spend ten or twenty years in a Zen monastery to achieve true *satori*.

The drug movement says to the churches: "Here, at last, *this* is what we were looking for, and never finding. This is what people really want. What do you have to offer in its place?" And so orthodoxy and the psychedelic experience arrive at their collision point.

The institutional challenge is serious, if you accept the premise that psychedelic experience is actually mystical experience. Obviously the churches cannot compete with the drugs in promoting that experience, even if they wished to. It remains to be asked whether the experience should be promoted— whether in fact it threatens a jet-age Quietism—and there are arguments on both sides, to be discussed later. But what about the doctrinal challenge? Is it really true that the central drug experience confirms the Eastern ideas we have mentioned? And why do these ideas have so much appeal for Westerners in this day and age?

To begin with, psychedelic experience is closer to Zen than it is to anything else the East has to offer. And Zen is a unique religion, even in the East. It appears to be monistic and pantheistic, but actually it is not. Unlike Hinduism, it does not indulge in elaborate metaphysics; as far as possible it avoids words altogether, and the student is advised to let the mildew grow on his lips. Basically anti-intellectual, Zen stresses intuition and the direct personal experience of reality. As Suzuki put it, Zen seeks only to grasp "the central fact of life," which is found only in the here and now. It is aimed at those "who die of hunger while sitting beside the rice bag." Unlike other schools of Buddhism, it does not regard the world as illusory, an epiphenomenon of the mind; like Saint Thomas, it rejects any dichotomy between body and spirit (as it rejects all other dualistic concepts): in essence it is a yes-saying to life and to the world. Suzuki was at pains to refute the idea that Zen is pantheistic. Zen neither confirms nor denies a transcendent God—another dualism—and if Zen seems strangely silent about God, that is only because all statements are limiting. If asked what God is, however, a Zen master might say, "Three pounds of flax." And this sounds pantheistic. If a Hindu said it, it would be pantheistic. But the Zen master's statement has nothing to do with such ideas; in calling attention to something quite prosaic, the Zen master is simply affirming the holiness of the commonplace in the moment being lived. He might just as easily have eaten a peach, gone for a walk—or slapped his pupil in the face again. Since *satori* can hardly be distinguished from the psychedelic experience, it is significant that Zen scholarship has not found in this insight any necessary implication of pantheism or monism; since Zen scholarship represents centuries of study devoted to the very subject which concerns them, immanence-minded drug cultists might find cause to re-examine their experience in the light of Zen.

Still, the sense of immanence under psychedelic influence is very pronounced. It is overwhelming. And after all, as we have already said, it is not necessary for an orthodox Westerner to reject the concept altogether: it is possible to conceive of God as both transcendent *and* immanent. To borrow an example which has been used before, Shakespeare is immanent in the characters of *The Tempest.* In him they live and move and have their Being. But Shakespeare also transcends his characters, in the sense that they do not exhaust his Being; the characters are Shakespeare, but Shakespeare is something more than Prospero and Trinculo.

In the same sense, the indwelling God acts from within, "through the path of immanence." He still transcends the world. But the world might fail to recognize this. The very fact of immanence could well blind men to God's transcendent character: in the psychedelic state especially, the part could easily mistake itself for the whole. As Baudelaire saw it, the hashish eater imagines himself to be God—and never thinks to ask himself the haunting question, "Might there not be another God?" Or to put it another way, "Might there not be *more* God?" Thus the psychedelic experience neither absolutely confirms nor absolutely denies God's transcendence. If it confirms anything, it confirms his immanence. And there is nothing in the experience which necessarily rules out an immanent God who is also transcendent.

Just as different ages have emphasized either the mystical or the rational aspect of religion, so too have immanence and transcendence been in and out of fashion. Saint Thomas, as might be expected, had attempted in his time to avoid either one extreme or the other, offering instead a synthesis of immanence and transcendence. Calvinism, on the other hand, insisted upon a majestic and omnipotent God who utterly transcended the pitiful race of man, and transcendence also was central to the Deism of Voltaire and others for whom God was the Great Watchmaker: having created the world and its laws, he had gone off to exist in complete isolation from his creation. The mystics for their part preached the immanence of God; throughout history, in fact, whenever orthodoxy has made God too remote and austere, the mystic prophets have appeared from the wilderness to reassert his immanence, and respect for immanence has gone hand in hand with an emphasis upon inner experience in religious devotion. Immanentist concepts were given powerful expression in the eighteenth and nineteenth centuries, both in literature and philosophy. But the first part of the twentieth century saw the emergence of a kind of neo-Calvinism, and Karl Barth again was in large part responsible for the development: his objection to mysticism necessarily included a concomitant objection to mysticism's accent on immanence, and the result was a renewed appreciation of divine transcendence.

It is possible, however, that the neglect of immanence has been at least partly to blame for the decline of religious enthusiasm in this era of technology and secularization. A wholly transcendent God is probably least compatible with modern science and modern experience—he is the kind of God modern man finds hardest to accept—and it does the churches no good to argue that this kind of God is a caricature. It does no good to insist that the churches have not preached this kind of God, and it does no good to argue that theology perhaps has proposed an entirely different kind of God. Doubtless we give theology and philosophy much more credit than they deserve. A great philosopher decides something, and we imagine that he has decided for his entire generation, if not for the century in which he lived; this school of opinion gives way to that school of opinion, and we suppose that mankind has been following the contest like a football match, with critical interest, and that everybody knows whether this side or that side has the ball at the moment. If the players would look around, however, they would find that the crowd is not paying much attention to the game, or does not understand it, or finds it hard to keep an eye on the ball. Of course the wholly transcendent God is a caricature—but a caricature by definition is a distortion or exaggeration of an actual characteristic, and an emphasis on transcendence has been a characteristic of Western theology. Indeed, this characteristic has mainly served to distinguish Western from Eastern religion, and it should hardly surprise us to find that a desire to preserve that distinction has led to an undue emphasis upon it in the public mind. "Do you believe in God?" Ask the common man that question, and he will assume you are referring to a transcendent figure of some sort. Ask the uncommon man the same question; he still will assume that *you* are referring to something along those lines. Of course he knows better, but he takes it for granted that you do not, when you ask the question. He may say, "Well, that depends what you mean by God." The question itself has come to imply that caricature of caricatures, the bearded monarch on the marble throne—and that image is inferred even in those cases when it is not actually implied. Especially is it inferred when the word God is spoken from the pulpit of a church. The idea is ridiculous, of course, and that is precisely the reason modern man no longer believes in it. Unfortunately, he still thinks he is being asked to believe in it, and that is the root of the problem. Eastern philosophy, on the other hand, does not ask him to believe in it, nor does the psychedelic experience ask him to believe in it, and the credit both give to immanence is without question responsible for much of the current interest in Eastern ideas and in LSD.

The churches had been complacent. Perhaps they imagined that the caricature no longer existed, and so they made no effort to correct it or to offer their parishioners a more plausible alternative. But the caricature did exist, although few people believed in it—or in anything else for that matter, as a direct consequence. The continued existence of the caricature resulted inevitably in a reaction against it, and necessarily in a drastic reaction. The idea was so deeply embedded in popular theology, and churchmen were so ignorant of this fact, that Altizer had to kill off the transcendent God altogether before the churchmen displayed any visible signs of alarm. Then LSD came along. If they now hope to preserve any vestige of transcendence, the churches might be well advised to take a fresh look at the weight of their teaching—and start talking immanence.

With the decline of Barthianism, this has already happened in radical theology. Basic to contemporary developments in this area have been the concept of immanence and the direct inner experience of that immanence. In Protestantism the reaction against stark transcendence can be traced progressively from Tillich to the New Theologians to the Death of God theologians. In Judaism the voice of Martin Buber has been heard. In Roman Catholicism immanence is the very heart of Teilhard de Chardin's theology.

But immanence has always been a dangerous idea, as we have indicated. Open the door to immanence and pantheism tries to slip in with it. This too has been happening.

9 The New Theology

A coffee shop in Indiana did not seem a very likely place in which to encounter the Anglican bishop of Woolwich, England, probably the best-known advocate of the radical New Theology. But that in fact is where I met him one dreary morning in 1966, on the Crawfordsville campus of Wabash College. Bishop John A. T. Robinson had come to Wabash from England to participate in the annual Lilly Lecture Series, and he looked a bit weary as he sat there in a corner booth discussing Dr. Thomas J. J. Altizer's announcement of God's demise. He shook his head over the idea, wondering aloud how Altizer could justify his curious position on Judaism. Later we left the shop together, heading for Robinson's temporary digs at the Caleb Mills House, and the balding, pink-cheeked bishop seemed a lonely figure as he walked across the campus through a misty rainfall, his macintosh flapping in the wind. Some three years before, with the publication of a little book titled *Honest to God,* he had been attacked as a heretic, a traitor to the faith and a false prophet; now—bitter pill—there were some who regarded him as a theological square: in fact a real cube. For the moment at least, the Ground of Being was Out. The Death of God was In.

Honest to God had created a sensation when it first appeared in 1963. To the astonishment of the author and his publishers, no doubt, the book became an international best seller, and total sales had exceeded a million when I met the bishop. There are as many New Theologies as there are New Theologians, but Robinson's book has had a tremendous impact both in Europe and America, and it offers an excellent vantage point from which to explore the main trends in radical theology just prior to the emergence of the Death of God school. It is in a sense a compendium of the ideas that shaped those trends, and what it did basically was bring together a number of concepts developed by four contemporary giants of philosophy and theology: Rudolf Bultmann, Dietrich Bonhoeffer, Paul Tillich, and Martin Buber. But it brought them together in a new synthesis, the most important aspect of which was a new interpretation of divine transcendence, and it popularized them for a vast lay readership. In doing so, it gave expression to the spiritual unrest and dissatisfaction of laymen who had been theologically inarticulate, and it helped also to lay a popular groundwork for the still more radical ideas which were soon to follow in America.

From Rudolf Bultmann, to begin with, the bishop took the concept of "demythologizing" the Bible.

To demythologize does not mean to debunk. On the contrary. A myth may represent an eternal truth—intuitively grasped perhaps—but the mode of expression will be dictated always by the world-view of the men who lived in the age when the myth was promulgated, and it will reflect also that age's level of knowledge and sophistication. Its language is metaphorical and anthropomorphic. The method of demythologizing probes for the deeper meaning hidden by the metaphor. "Its aim," said Bultmann, "is not to eliminate the mythological statements but to interpret them." In essence this is the same test we applied in an earlier chapter to Wordsworth's ode and to poetic symbolism in general: does the *"is"* really mean *"is,"* or does it perhaps mean *"as if"*? Suppose, then, said Bultmann, that the authors of the Bible wanted to convey the idea of God's transcendence. They could do so only by resorting to the crude category of space—resulting in a God who is "up there" in a place called heaven. According to Robinson, a more sophisticated age refined the veridical myth to connote a God who was not "up there" but "out there," somewhere beyond the flashing comets. But again this is a crude metaphor, and it no longer satisfies modern man, who is intruding upon outer space with radio telescopes and rocket probes. To remain relevant, the truth of God's transcendence must be demythologized or de-metaphorized. It and other biblical truths must be retranslated in modern terms for men who are able to digest deeper levels of abstraction. But how? If God is not "up there" or "out there," where is he?

From Dietrich Bonhoeffer, the bishop took the concept of a Christianity "without religion." This is certainly an enigmatic idea, and Bonhoeffer never had an opportunity to elaborate upon it; it was merely suggested in letters and notes which he wrote in a Nazi prison before he was hanged in April 1945. But it has haunted many churchmen with a moth-to-flame

fascination, and it would be difficult to exaggerate the fundamental influence it has had upon contemporary theology. For
most New Theologians it has served as a sort of Rorschach ink
blot, and each has brought to it his own interpretation. For
Robinson it represented at one level a rejection of churchiness
and otherworldliness. God is neither "up there" nor "out
there." He is rather, in Bonhoeffer's words, "the 'beyond' in
the midst of our life." And that is where we should seek him,
in our midst.

Traditionally, said Robinson, religion has implied withdrawal
from the world to a special compartment of life where, in a sort
of spiritual vacuum, one prays and thinks holy thoughts. Too
often, in Ronald Gregor Smith's phrase, it has implied "a kind
of battle against the world on behalf of God." One seeks God
only in the sanctuary, in the gaps of life. Inevitably, this attitude
has made worship possible, or profitable, for only a compara-
tively small cadre of religiously minded people—for the praying
type. And something else. If God is used simply as a *deus ex
machina* to explain man's unanswered questions about life and
the universe, what happens when these questions, one after one,
are answered? God is pushed further and further back by the
tidal advance of knowledge, said Bonhoeffer. Man has less and
less need of him. "As in the scientific field," said Bonhoeffer,
"so in human affairs generally, what we call 'God' is being more
and more edged out of life, losing more and more ground.
Catholic and Protestant historians are agreed that it is in this
development that the great defection from God, from Christ, is
to be discerned." Indeed, Robinson agreed, Julian Huxley expressed the same idea or was thinking in the same vein when he
observed that, operationally, God "is beginning to resemble
not a ruler but the last fading smile of a cosmic Cheshire Cat."

The world has come of age, said Bonhoeffer, and men in a world come of age should accept their adulthood; they should go about their business just *as if* God did not exist, not clinging to his hand every time there is a street to cross. "God allows himself to be edged out of the world, and that is exactly the way, the only way, in which he can be with us and help us." Like a parent who wants his child to be self-reliant.

But how does one worship in a post-religious world? By accepting the world, said Robinson. By seeking the sacred in the secular, the holy in the common, the beyond in our midst. One should seek God "in the hungry, the naked, the homeless and the prisoner." Prayer should not be a withdrawal from the world to God but a penetration through the world to God; for nothing, after all, is really secular: the whole world is holy.

From Paul Tillich, the bishop took the concept of defining God as the Ground of Being. Tillich rejected the view that God is in any sense *a* Being. This rejection applies of course to the God of Deism, who started the world ticking with mechanistic precision and then went off somewhere far away and remote, very much, as Robinson put it, "like a rich aunt in Australia." But Tillich also rejected the more familiar God of Theism, in so far as that implies some kind of supernatural Person—a separate Being who exists in an intimate relationship with the world which he transcends. Theism necessarily does imply this kind of God, said Tillich. It implies "a being beside others" who is simply a part of reality—the most important part, but still only a part; it implies that God "is a being, not being-itself." Tillich proposed that theology replace this Being with the Ground of Being, and that a new dimension be adopted to conceptualize this reality. As a substitute for height (as in "up there") or distance (as in "out there"), Tillich suggested that we think of God in terms of depth (as in "in our midst").

Robinson took up the suggestion, defining God as "the ultimate depth of all our being, the creative ground and meaning of all our existence."

The bishop wrote that traditional Christian theology has concerned itself with adducing proofs for the existence of God, and the psychological implication, at least, is that God might not exist.

Well, then, what happens if we speak of God simply as ultimate reality or the Ground of our Being—as opposed, for example, to *a* Being?

Then it is no longer necessary to debate the existence of God, since nobody doubts there is an ultimate reality. The whole problem is reduced to speculation about the *nature* of this ultimate reality, or God.

A lot of people didn't like that. It seemed much too easy, for one thing. And perhaps there is a basic flaw in the argument, as we shall see later. In any case, the bishop also used the Ground of Being as a wedge for the most awesome effort of all —demythologizing God himself. Behind the various mythological expressions, what is the ontology of God? What is the nature of ultimate reality, and what in truth is the real meaning of transcendence?

From Martin Buber, the bishop took the concept of the I-Thou relationship. We have already referred to this concept; let us examine it now in more detail. Buber was a mystic, and he began his argument with the proposition that all men are born with a sense of cosmic connection. The sense of "I" or individual self is not present at birth, and in fact the child at first does not distinguish between himself and the shining world which his eyes have opened upon. In the womb he had known a life "of purely natural combination, bodily interaction and flowing one to the other," and after birth he still rests for a time "in the womb of the great mother, the undivided primal world that precedes form." Buber recalled the saying of the Jews: "In the mother's body man knows the universe, in birth he forgets it." But he does not forget it all at once, and he never forgets it completely. Before his sense of natural connection with the world fades gradually away, the child is given time to establish a sense of spiritual connection—which Buber referred to as relation. Gradually there develops a sense of "I" or self— "the separation of the body from the world round about it"—but the world nevertheless is still perceived as existing in relation to the self. It is perceived as Thou, and this is the I-Thou relationship. But the sense of "I" grows ever stronger, until at last it snaps the fragile bond of relation between subject and object, I and Thou. Thou becomes It (or He or She), and I-It is the primary word of separation.

The world perceived as It is something to be used and exploited, and it is perceived in space and time—whereas the world as Thou is not perceived in space and time. The world perceived as It is chopped into isolated segments, and the segments are ranked in an artificial order; they are organized for cause-and-effect analysis, so that man can "get his bearings." Man no longer looks at the world in relation: "instead of looking at it he observes it, instead of accepting it as it is, he turns it to his own account." And why? "Only as It can it enter the structure of knowledge." This is necessary for survival, because man cannot live without It. "But he who lives with It alone is not a man," and the memory of Thou never dies altogether: there are "short, uncanny moments" when it reappears, "lyric and dramatic episodes, seductive and magical." The memory of that undivided primal world lingers as "a secret image of desire," and Buber implied that this is the real meaning of the Freudian wish to retreat to the womb. Not at all the sign of an unhealthy pathology, it represents a natural longing to re-establish the cosmic connection. Man of course cannot crawl back into the womb, in this life at least, but he can relate to the world; he can look for the thing-in-itself, seeing "each thing simply as being." He can say "Thou" to the world, and the world in turn will say "Thou" back to him. In this relationship a man affirms the reality of the world—and he affirms also the reality of himself. For the "I" is very real. With the emergence of personal life, a man cannot deny his "I," but he can choose what sort of "I" it will be—since the "I" of I-Thou is not the same as the "I" of I-It. A man can choose to be a *person* or an *individual,* and all men are either persons or individuals: the "I" of I-Thou is a person, and the "I" of I-It is an individual. In I-Thou a man does not and cannot surrender his personality, since the essence of I-Thou is personal relation: an "I" relating to the Thou. A person does not lose "his special being, his being different." But he does not revel in his special being as the individual does; he simply accepts it as a necessary part of being in general. He seeks for the Thou, which he sees in the eyes of every man and every creature. He lives in the here and now, fully aware that "the one thing that matters is visible, full acceptance of the present." He recognizes that true love is the "responsibility of an I for a Thou," and this leads him at last "to the dreadful point—to love all men." He hallows this life, and thus he meets the living God who is present in every relational event. In every finite Thou he catches a glimpse of the eternal Thou.

I-Thou was the final ingredient in Robinson's eclectic omelet;

he was ready now to face the question of God—and the question of God, he acknowledged, was the question of transcendence. It was certainly the question as far as the Western God was concerned—no doubt about that—and the bishop therefore did his best to salvage the concept. That really was the whole point of his book, although many of his critics received just the opposite impression. The task, he said, was "to validate the idea of transcendence for modern man."

Robinson began with an all-out attack on Theistic transcendence, agreeing with Tillich that the atheists were quite correct in rejecting a transcendent Being or supreme Person. The bishop conceded the fact that classical Christian theology does not in fact picture God as a Person, and "the Church's best theologians have not laid themselves open to such attack." Nevertheless, he said, "popular Christianity has always posited such a supreme personality," and the question really was whether or not popular theology could afford to sacrifice the concept. To do so, R. W. Hepburn had written, "seems at once to take one quite outside Christianity." Robinson felt, however, that the concept could be abandoned—indeed it *must* be, since the average layman was finding it harder and harder to take seriously. People must be told, then, that there is no reason they should take it seriously. "If Christianity is to survive . . . there is no time to lose in detaching it from this scheme of thought."

But to what does one attach it? To what does transcendence refer, if not to a transcendent Being?

Robinson groped for an answer. And he found one, he thought, in man's divine attributes—love, wisdom, justice. Feuerbach was looking over his shoulder now, and the bishop knew he was treading "on very dangerous ground." One slip and he could easily plunge into the bottomless chasm of hu-

133

manism or pantheism, making of man's nature the *ens realis-simum*. The problem perhaps was to identify God as the source of our higher aspirations, without at the same time making us synonymous with the source—that is to say, without making man and God identical. In any case, the bishop pushed on with the idea of defining God as the Ground of our Being or as ultimate reality. If God is ultimate reality, what, then, is this ultimate reality? Tillich had proposed that we think of it in terms of depth, you will remember, and Robinson quoted Tillich's seminal passage:

> The name of this infinite and inexhaustible depth and ground of all being is *God*. That depth is what the word *God* means. And if that word has not much meaning for you, translate it, and speak of the depths of your life, of the source of your being, of your ultimate concern, of what you take seriously without any reservation. Perhaps, in order to do so, you must forget everything traditional that you have learned about God, perhaps even that word itself. For if you know that God means depth, you know much about him. You cannot then call yourself an atheist or unbeliever. For you cannot think or say: Life has no depth! Life is shallow. [Furthermore] . . . speak of the depth of history, of the ground and aim of our social life, and of what you take seriously without reservation in your moral and political activities. Perhaps you should call this depth *hope,* simply hope.

One is reminded also of Tillich's "courage to be" as an argument for faith. Why this courage? Where does it come from? In the same sense, why do men hope—and where does their hope originate if not in the very depths of their Being?

In the last analysis, depth meant for Tillich "those deep things for which religion stands: the feeling for the inexhaustible mystery of life, the grip of an ultimate meaning of existence." And this mystery—this ultimate meaning—is the source of the biblical intuition that there is *something* which transcends our everyday life and the world of appearances. There is, to use a cliche, more here than meets the eye. And this "more" is the transcendent—the not seen. It is that which we normally do not perceive or recognize, but which nevertheless makes such urgent demands upon us. It is the truth about ourselves and the truth about Being itself. "To call God transcendent in this sense," said Tillich, "does not mean that one must establish a 'superworld' of divine objects. It does mean that, within itself, the finite world points beyond itself. In other words, it is self-transcendent." As Robinson expressed it: "The necessity for the name 'God' lies in the fact that our being has depths which naturalism, whether evolutionary, mechanistic, dialectical or humanistic, cannot or will not recognize." And in Tillich's words again: "We are always held and comprehended by something that is greater than we are, that has a claim upon us, and that demands response from us." This is the Ground of our Being, and we can no more escape it than Francis Thompson could escape the Hound of Heaven. A trumpet sounds from the hid battlements of Eternity, and a Voice declares: "All things betray thee, who betrayest Me . . . Naught shelters thee, who wilt not shelter Me . . . Lo! naught contents thee, who content'st not Me."

To thine own Self be true. Is that what this means? Is that what God means?

At Wabash I had a long talk with Robinson in the library of the Caleb Mills House, and I asked him, among other things,

"However that word God is finally translated, do you believe that it transcends our Being?" He replied, "Yes. I believe, obviously, that God represents a reality which in a real sense encounters us as it were from without. It is not something that we think up for ourselves. In many ways I would find it much easier to invent a very different kind of God, far less uncomfortable to live with. There is this, I think, overmastering reality which challenges us, judges us, confronts us, questions our whole being. It is this element of otherness—of unconditional grace and demand—which it seems to me traditional Christianity has meant by transcendence. This is a dimension of experience in life which I've no desire whatever to deny. What I am concerned with is to try and find some way of expressing this dimension which doesn't put God right at the edge of our whole experience and world."

An unconditional demand would seem to imply a built-in demand which is forced upon us by the very nature of our Being. It would seem to imply that we are not completely free to choose our own destiny and to make of ourselves whatever we please. Or, to put it another way—and the distinction is important—we *are* free to choose, but our freedom is less than perfect: if we deny the unconditional demand, we will suffer for it. We will suffer the anguish of alienation from the Ground of our Being. To boil it down, Sartre was wrong. There is an essence (unconditional) which precedes our existence and which gives our existence its meaning and direction; it tells us what we should do and where we should go. Whether we heed it or not is up to us.

But what is this essence? What is the Ground of our Being? What is ultimate reality?

In three words, what is God?

In his book, Robinson used three words to answer those questions. And he took the three words from another book. To understand his meaning, we must return for a moment to Buber, to whom the bishop owes a large debt, and we must ask what Buber meant by the eternal Thou, as opposed simply to Thou.

Buber had no objection to the word God. Anticipating what was to come, perhaps, he wrote in *I and Thou,* first published in 1923: "Many men wish to reject the word God as a legitimate usage, because it is so misused. It is indeed the most heavily laden of all the words used by men. For that very reason it is the most imperishable and most indispensable." Buber had no sympathy with the Eastern concept of absorption in the Absolute, in "the One thinking Essence." He spoke of relation, not absorption. He opposed the doctrine that "universal being and self-being are the same." He told of a Face that is sometimes seen, briefly, when one looks deep into the eyes of a finite Thou. This is God, the eternal Thou. And this is transcendent. "Every sphere is compassed in the eternal Thou, but it is not compassed in them." "God comprises, but is not, the universe. So too, God comprises, but is not, my Self." Nor did Buber refrain from speaking of God as a Person; in a 1957 postscript to his book, he wrote:

> The description of God as a Person is indispensable for everyone who like myself means by "God" not a principle (although mystics like Eckhart sometimes identify him with "Being") and like myself means by "God" not an idea (although philosophers like Plato at times could hold that he was this): but who rather means by "God," as I do, him who—whatever else he may be—enters into a direct relation with us men in creative, revealing and redeeming

acts, and thus makes it possible for us to enter into a direct relation with him. This ground and meaning of our existence constitutes a mutuality, arising again and again, such as can subsist only between persons. The concept of personal being is indeed completely incapable of declaring what God's essential being is, but it is both permitted and necessary to say that God is *also* a Person. . . . From this attribute would stem my and all men's being as person . . . As a Person God gives personal life, he makes us as persons become capable of meeting with him and with one another. But no limitation can come upon him as the absolute Person, either from us or from our relations with one another; in fact we can dedicate to him not merely our persons but also our relations to one another.

Buber conceded that there was an apparent contradiction in the concept of God as an Absolute Person who cannot be limited and the assertion that his total Being is in fact limited "by the plurality of other independent entities" (namely, us). It is possible that Buber here was addressing himself to Tillich's criticism of the Theistic God who is only a part of reality, "a being beside others." Buber said, however, that this was not really a contradiction: it was a paradox. And he added the enigmatic statement: "It is as the absolute Person that God enters into direct relation with us. The contradiction yields to deeper insight."

Robinson in his book referred to Buber only in passing, as it were, and did not give him equal billing with Bultmann, Bonhoeffer, and Tillich as a major source of inspiration. Wedded as he was to Tillich's denial of Theism, the bishop certainly did not refer his readers to the passage we have cited on God as a

Person. Nevertheless, his final conclusions about God or ultimate reality might very well appear to be a liberal interpretation of that passage, based perhaps on a "deeper insight." At Wabash I mentioned to Robinson that his concept of transcendence seemed to have a strong streak of Buber in it, and the bishop agreed. "I think what Buber is saying is fundamental," he said. "And in fact this goes back a long way in my own theological experience, because I did my Ph.D. thesis on Martin Buber, which has never been published. This was twenty to twenty-five years ago. And therefore this represents a long-standing influence on my thinking. And I think the kind of thing Buber is trying to get at in this I-Thou relationship—the way he sees every finite Thou as a sort of glimpse through, a 'window through' into something which meets us in, with, and under every relationship of life—this is very near the heart of what I am trying to say."

Did Robinson in fact demythologize Buber? Was Buber in fact asking to be demythologized? What might it be, that "deeper insight"?

Although he rejected the idea that God is a Person, the bishop did affirm that God is *personal*. This may appear contradictory at first reading, but we must remember that Robinson was speaking of God as ultimate reality—as the truth about existence. "For this way of thinking," he wrote, "to say that 'God is personal' is to say that 'reality at its very deepest level is personal,' that personality is of *ultimate* significance in the constitution of the universe, that in personal relationships we touch the final meaning of existence as nowhere else." And he quoted Feuerbach: "To predicate personality of God is nothing else than to predicate personality as the absolute essence."

But personality in itself is not yet the absolute essence. If it is only in personal relationships that we touch the final meaning of existence, what, then, is that final meaning? What, then, is God? The bishop now was prepared to answer the question.

God, he said, is love.

"To assert that 'God is love' is to believe that in love one comes into touch with the most fundamental reality in the universe, that Being itself ultimately has this character."

This is the "more" which does not meet the eye. This is the truth about ourselves and the truth about Being itself. This is the unconditional demand that is made of us: that we love one another. And this truth, this ultimate reality, we have objectivized as God. But God as love does not imply "a super-Being beyond the world endowed with personal qualities." No. "To believe in God as love means to believe that in pure personal relationship we encounter, not merely what ought to be, but what is, the deepest, veriest truth about the structure of reality." It means to believe that love is the Ground of our Being. It means that "theological statements are not a description of 'the highest Being' but an analysis of the depths of personal relationships."

The bishop continued: "A statement is 'theological' not because it relates to a particular Being called 'God' but because it asks *ultimate* questions about the meaning of existence: it asks what, at the level of *theos,* at the level of its deepest mystery, is the reality and significance of our life." And this reality, this final truth, this God is love.

Who, then, was Jesus—the son of God?

Robinson demythologized him, too. Jesus was not a God-man who came from "out there," pretending to be a man. He was not a divine visitant who chose to live "like one of the natives." According to the bishop, the traditional view of Jesus leaves one with the impression that "God took a space ship and arrived on this planet in the form of a man." It leaves the impression that Jesus "was not really one of us . . . he came from outside." And that word incarnation: in itself, it "conjures up the idea of a divine substance being plunged in flesh and coated with it like chocolate or silver plating." But Jesus in fact was a man; he was in fact one of us.

Nevertheless, Jesus also revealed to the world the Word of God. He was a man, yes—but a man who was completely united with the Ground of his Being. He made himself "utterly transparent" to the Ground of Being and thus offered his fellow-men a window through to ultimate reality. He did this by emptying himself of self; he was "the man for others," and his whole life was a testimony to the fact that the Ground of all Being is love. I asked the bishop whether the I-Thou relation did not imply that *all* men are a window through to the eternal Thou—hadn't Buber in fact said the same thing about a cat?—and Robinson answered:

"Can I just say two things? First, this window-through metaphor is obviously very inadequate and just suggests that God is there to be looked at, whereas the New Testament takes a far more dynamic view. I mean, here in a real sense is the activity and love and purpose of God being revealed and poured out and acting through this man's life. The second question relates to the uniqueness of Christ. I think I certainly would not want to say that he is unique in the sense that he is quite abnormal. I think that it's worth asking: Is Christ unique because he is normal, or because he is abnormal? Now, I think a great many people would take from the Gospels as they read them today that he is unique because he is abnormal—in the sense that he did all kinds of things we couldn't do, was born in an entirely different way, had all kinds of miraculous powers, and so on. Well now, if that is the picture of Christ, then he seems to me a man who has very little to do with our life at all. It seems to me what the New Testament fundamentally is saying is that here is someone who is uniquely normal, what all human life should be, what a genuinely human existence ought to be. And, on the whole, this is not true of any other man—we are in a real sense failing to be what we were meant to be. Now, in that sense I would certainly say that Christ is unique. But I don't think he's unique in a sense that cuts him off from the whole of the rest of humanity. And one of the troubles about so much of the mythological view of the New Testament is that, for man today, its effect is to sever this person from everybody else. After all, the New Testament itself talks about Christ as the firstborn of many brothers—meaning that there's a real solidarity here with the whole of the rest of humanity—and I don't want to draw his uniqueness in any sense which denies this solidarity, but rather to say that he is the uniquely normal human being."

In his book Robinson ridiculed supernatural interpretations of the Atonement—the idea that a divine Person descended from heaven to save men from sin "in the way that a man might put his finger into a glass of water to rescue a struggling insect." He suggested that sin and hell are metaphors for man's estrangement from the Ground of his Being, while union with the Ground of Being "is the meaning of heaven," and the experience of grace is the experience of being accepted in that heaven where, in Tillich's words, "everything is transformed." On the level of worship, the bishop called for a "worldly holiness" and a "sacred secularity" in which the beyond is sought at the center of life, "between man and man"—for God is discovered only in the here and now, in the concrete moment, in personal relationships: he is not discovered in some other world, nor is he to be found in the self alone. Finally, the New Theologian proposed a New Morality—a modern ethic, based on the Ground of Being, which would take as its credo Saint Augustine's injunction: "Love God, and do what you like." He even suggested that premarital sex might be wrong only in ninety-nine cases out of a hundred, arguing that "the only intrinsic evil is lack of love." In an age that was turning its back on supernatural legalism, he said, he was only trying to offer a reasonable system, founded on the absolute priority of love, which could answer that troublesome question, "Why not?" Thus a boy would not take liberties with a girl unless he loved her; and if he loved her, he would not take liberties with her. Or so it seemed to the bishop. (See his book *Christian Morals Today*.)

Robinson warned his readers not to equate the eternal Thou with the finite Thou, "nor God with man or nature." This, he pointed out, would be pantheism or humanism, and "Christianity must challenge the assumption of naturalism that God is merely a redundant name for nature or for humanity." With Tillich, he said, he wished instead to push beyond both supernaturalism *and* naturalism; it was not his intention, he said, "to substitute an immanent for a transcendent Deity," but rather to reaffirm transcendence in a new translation. The bishop attempted to demonstrate, therefore, that his position was not the same as humanism on the one hand or pantheism on the other.

To rebut the charge of humanism, he returned to his statement that God is love; this could not be turned around, he said, to imply that love is God. In other words, divine love is not simply a projection of human love; on the contrary, human love is a projection of divine love: it occurs on this earth because love is the Ground of Being. We recognize human love as sacred because we see in it the ultimate truth about reality; we see in it "the divine agape of the universe." We love because the Ground of our Being demands that we love. This demand upon us is unconditional—beyond our control as individuals—and therefore it transcends us. And this element of transcendence is what finally distinguishes the humanist from the radical Christian. The humanist says love *ought* to be the final truth about existence; the radical Christian says it *is*. Furthermore, the radical Christian says that this final truth is revealed to us in Jesus Christ, and its validity "stands or falls" with that revelation. So this in turn is what finally distinguishes both radical and orthodox Christianity from all other theologies, Eastern and Western—and, we might add, from the psychedelic cults.

Turning to the next charge, the bishop conceded that his rejection of Theism might raise in some minds the specter of the Eastern God. He acknowledged that it was dangerous to abandon the concept of God as a separate Being. Indeed, he said, traditionalists might find it hard to believe that his position "must not result in a theology of mere immanence, not to say of pantheism." But, he said, there was one element which ultimately distinguished his view from the pantheistic or immanentist position—and this was the element of personal freedom: the freedom of the individual person to accept or deny the Ground of his Being. Pantheism is purely mechanistic or deterministic; concern for the other is as automatic as two plus two, since in fact there is no other but only the monistic One, and this concern cannot properly be described as love, which is a relationship between persons and not the Selfish awareness of an Absolute Identity. For example, you are concerned for the welfare of your arms and legs, but you would hardly refer to this concern as love. I am extrapolating now—trying to read the bishop's mind, as it were—but I trust this is close to his meaning. The "I" is real, as is the Thou, but the two are bound together by God. And God is love. This is what it means to say that God is personal but not a Person. Love is the very Ground of our Being; but so too is independence an essential aspect of our Being: indeed it must be, if love is also, for the one implies the other.

Extrapolating again, it might be suggested that we worship not God—the word itself would seem to indicate a Person—but rather perhaps a symbolic X. Maybe we should offer up our prayers to Love, which in fact is what we do. All day long the radio blares the message, flooding our homes and our autos with songs of love and little else—news, sports, and love: that is the prescribed formula—and our literature, too, seems preoccupied with the theme. Some call it sex; but is it really God? What sends the unhappy young man wandering the lonely streets of night in search of Her? Is it God who sends him, the Ground of his Being? If God is love we are a pious nation.

We shall not belabor the possible parallels between Robinson's demythologized Christianity and many of the Eastern or psychedelic concepts we have already discussed. They should be obvious. What especially stands out, of course, is the idea of immanence, and the reader will decide for himself whether the bishop has managed to slam the door in time. Or has pantheism slipped in? To many it may appear that the bishop is hanging by his fingernails over those chasms we mentioned, as far as transcendence is concerned, and it would be worthwhile to take one last look at his definition of this term.

It seems fair to say that Robinson has made the term

transcendent synonymous with the term *unconditional*. Love is a built-in aspect of existence; it is not ours to command; it is the essence which precedes our existence; it is the "more" which does not meet the eye and which does not yield itself to the scrutiny of an empirical science. As the bishop put it to me: "Here is something before which you say, yes, this is it. Here I stand, I can no other. I think this *is* something in a real sense that confronts one, engages one, from outside. It's not something one thinks up for oneself. It clearly, as I see it, is describing how things *are*. You say, well, here is something fundamentally true which I cannot escape." For example perhaps, one does not think up breathing for oneself.

But some critics might argue that an unconditional "more" is not really the same as a transcendent "other," and "in a real sense" is, after all, a deceptive phrase; it sounds positive, but actually it weakens and modifies more than it reinforces—that is to say, it implies *"as if,"* not *"is."* It is significant that the bishop did not say simply: "This is something that confronts one from outside." Because he did not say this, and probably could not, it is debatable whether Robinson was successful in his effort to validate transcendence for popular theology, since transcendence has always implied "outside," "other," or "separate," and the bishop's God displays none of these qualities. It is not enough to say this God transcends the individual, since transcendence has always implied something more than just this; it has implied a divinity that transcends mankind as a whole—and not in the sense of being unconditional, but rather in the sense of being separate and superior (at least *partly* separate, and wholly superior).

Robinson of course was well aware of this, and it was precisely this implication he was trying to combat with his new definition. It might be argued that Robinson did not actually redefine transcendence; it might be argued that he substituted an altogether different concept. "Deep," for example, is not a redefinition of "tall," and unconditional, in this sense, is not a redefinition of transcendent. But this may be quibbling; substitution and redefinition shade into each other, and perhaps there *is* a sense in which the bishop's God "as it were" transcends us. ("As it were" is another of the bishop's favorite phrases.) If you think about it a long while, there will be moments when you say yes—and moments when you say no, or maybe. It is not an easy concept to get your mind around; it is, if you like, rather vague (or mysterious), and you will see perhaps why we objected to talk of a vague pantheism. Pantheism is very easy. By comparison, one can well appreciate the frustration of the critic who described Robinson as a confused man who is confusing others. There are, however, a great many people who would say that the bishop has provided them with something other than confusion. From one point of view, he may have taken away their silver—but returned them gold. In an era of subjective chaos, he has made religion meaningful again for untold thousands. While he may well have scuttled transcendence in its traditional interpretation—may indeed have lost it altogether—his system does retain the Western concept of pluralism. And this in the final test could prove to have more significance even than transcendence.

Perhaps the bishop himself has acknowledged this. You will recall the argument, derived from Tillich, that atheism collapses if you define God simply as ultimate reality. Then it is necessary to debate only the nature of this ultimate reality, the bishop said. And he added this: "One can only ask what ultimate reality is like—whether, for instance, in the last analysis what lies at the heart of things and governs their working is to be described in personal or impersonal categories." That perhaps is the real question, and not transcendence. That perhaps is the basis of the more fundamental challenge which is offered to the West by LSD and by Eastern metaphysics. The bishop of course took the position that ultimate reality is personal, and this is another way of saying that it is pluralistic: "love," "relation," "personal"—all these are pluralistic words, opposed to monism. They preserve the integrity both of Thou and "I." If God is love, he cannot be Atman. If God is personal, there is no One.

We have said, however, that the instant remedy for atheism contains within it a possible flaw. As Robinson saw it, "one cannot argue whether ultimate reality exists," and we have quoted Tillich's assertion: nobody can say or think that life has no depth, that life is shallow. But in fact men can and do assert that ultimate reality does not exist, that life is shallow and has no depth. Existence, some say, is absurd. Life is a joke —a rather ghastly one at that—and there is no ultimate reality in the sense of an unconditional purpose or meaning. For atheistic existentialists, such as Sartre, there is no Ground of Being, no unconditional, no primary state of Being in any sense; not only is there no God, there is no such thing even as a definite human nature, for existence precedes essence. And what does this mean? "It means," said Sartre, "that, first of all, man exists, turns up, appears on the scene, and, only afterward, defines himself." In the beginning is subjectivity. In the beginning, man is nothing. "Only afterward will he be something, and he himself will have made what he will be. . . . Man is nothing else but what he makes of himself." He must choose what he will be, and that terrible responsibility is his alone. Man, to his horror, is born free. He is, indeed, "condemned to be free." He is "condemned every moment to invent man." There are no determinisms. There is, said Sartre, "no human nature for me to depend on."

"We are alone, with no excuses."

Robinson perhaps recognized his own error, for he also wrote: "The question of God is the question whether this depth of being is a reality or an illusion." And the next question, then, is obvious.

True or false—how does one decide? How does one determine whether the Ground of Being is real or not?

There is first of all the possibility of rational proof. But those who hold to this possibility have had many centuries in which to produce their evidence, and the evidence has not been universally convincing.

There is next the possibility of revelation—and especially, for the bishop, the possibility of revelation through Jesus Christ. I asked Robinson *why* the radical Christian says that love is the final truth, as opposed to the humanist who says it ought to be, and the bishop said: "I think that this is defined and vindicated in Christ. And personally, unless I saw this in Christ, and really felt that this was the clue, then there are so many things in our modern world which would suggest otherwise that I should find it very difficult to hang on to this. But this is in a sense, I think, the sort of knot in the thread." But the knot was tied almost two thousand years ago, and there are signs today it is coming undone. The revelation existed when the modern world came into being, and men ever since have paid less and less heed to it. Today men have eyes to see, and they do not see; they have ears to hear, and they do not hear. Or so it might appear to the church at least.

"Often enough," said Buber, "we think there is nothing to hear, but long before we have ourselves put wax in our ears." So the problem perhaps is basic enough. How can men be made to look and see, listen and hear? How can the scales be removed from their eyes and the wax from their ears?

Robinson's solution was to demythologize, or redefine, and this for many has been richly rewarding. But is it enough? In itself, after all, it is rational analysis again—and this alone has never been enough. It may serve to illuminate or to justify a truth that has been intuitively perceived, however vaguely. But what if that perception was lacking to begin with? Are we not thrown back once more on the primary necessity for a direct inner experience of the ultimate reality, which is God and the Ground of our Being?

This issue is implicit in the New Theology's response to secularization. Many New Theologians have taken Bonhoeffer to mean that the church should turn exclusively to this world, becoming secular itself—that religion should be made "relevant" by involving it full scale in social and political issues, and, in a more shallow sense, by adapting it to contemporary mores and the modern idiom (beat prayers, jam sessions at the altar). But is this what people really want from religion? Or do they seek instead that intimate, personal encounter which in turn is the ultimate *basis* for social action? Are the secularizers putting the cart before the horse? In their reaction against otherworldliness, do they threaten a further diminution of that mystical element for which LSD seems to demonstrate a widespread hunger? There is no simple answer, but the problem is there. And so LSD perhaps challenges not only orthodoxy but also one aspect at least of radical theology.

Robinson himself is not limited to this one aspect; he is not to be identified with the secularizers alone—although Altizer has so identified him. Certainly he has a good deal of sympathy for this school, which derives largely from Bonhoeffer. But, as he put it to me, "There is a whole other side which I took over from Tillich, and there is a whole lot for instance in Teilhard de Chardin, and others, which I think is equally important." This other side, of course, represents the mystical-philosophical approach to theology—or, in other words, the metaphysical school. "What I'm trying to do," Robinson said, "is to combine this with the sort of thing that the prophets of secularization are saying, and I don't want to have to choose between them." The bishop indeed has shared Saint Thomas' penchant for synthesis—he has not been an either/or thinker, and this no doubt explains why some have thought him confused or confusing. While many of his basic viewpoints were drawn from mystical philosophy, however, and while mystics such as Tillich and Buber have been his own inspiration, the bishop in his book nevertheless took a dim view of mysticism for the average person, and of mysticism as a solution. He wrote:

> Our contention has been that God is to be met not by a "religious" turning away from the world but in unconditional concern for "the other" *seen through to its ultimate depths.* . . . That there are veridical experiences of the type usually called "mystical" or "religious" no one would be so foolish as to deny, and a man may thank God for them as St. Paul did for his visions. But the capacity for religious or mystical awareness, as for aesthetic or psychic awareness, is largely a question of natural endowment. Women, for instance, appear to be naturally more

religious—and more psychic—than men. To make the knowledge of God depend upon such experiences is like making it depend on an ear for music. There are those who are tone-deaf, and there are those who would not claim to have any clearly distinguishable "religious" experiences.

Again, in our own conversation, I asked Robinson if Bonhoeffer was not, among other things, rejecting what the bishop referred to as churchiness. "Yes," said Robinson. "He's also certainly rejecting any view of religion which sees it just as a compartment of life and sees the church as a sort of religious club for those who like that sort of thing—which indeed it very largely is. That is one of the troubles. It exists to meet the needs of religiously minded people—which seems to me a great distortion of the real function of the church, which is much more concerned with the making holy of the common, with the transformation of the whole of life, and not simply in providing the same sort of function that, say, a musical club does for those who like music."

Obviously, as the bishop has interpreted it, Bonhoeffer's rejection of "religion" is nothing more or less than a rejection of mysticism in the sense that we have defined it. The question remains, how does one manage to *see* the holy in the common, and how is the whole of life to *be* transformed unless there is, to begin with, some inner experience corresponding to a mystical awareness? You cannot simply tell people to see the holy, or point it out to them, and no New Theology, however radical, is going to transform the whole of life. If people cannot find ultimate reality in Jesus Christ, they are not going to find it in Tillich. It could be argued that more churchiness is just what is needed. Robinson of course had no intrinsic objection to mysticism; on the contrary, he was merely facing the fact that most people cannot achieve the state.

Or could not, the drug movement would say. If everybody in the world would take LSD tonight, under the proper conditions, it is possible that tomorrow there would be millions more of the praying type.

Here, then, in its full scope, is LSD's challenge to New Theology.

As for New Theology's own challenge to orthodoxy, the traditionalists have taken comfort in the fact that Robinson since publication of his book has more or less dropped that phrase Ground of Being. The idea seems to be that this was some sort of capitulation, and a collective sigh of relief was heard. Robinson indicated to me, however, that he had tended to "shear off" the phrase simply because "it obviously seems to cause so much misunderstanding." A great many people, he said, "have assumed this is a purely impersonal phrase and is the enemy of belief in God as in any sense a personal reality." That of course is not the way he interpreted it himself. I asked him if the book still stood, or if he had changed his viewpoint in any fundamental area. "I think basically it still stands," he said. He had not in fact read the book since it was last in proof. "But I wouldn't say that radically I have regretted anything I have written, or changed it."

When they were not denouncing him for heresy, the bishop's critics tried the opposite tack. After all, he was saying nothing more than the church itself had always said. It was old stuff. During a public debate at Wabash, for example, Professor J. V. Langmead Casserley of Seabury-Western Theological Seminary declared the bishop was "profoundly in

harmony with the deepest theological opinions of the church."
The bishop was being honest to God perhaps, but dishonest
to history. Well, the bishop never said his stuff was new. He
did say it was not being communicated—a fact attested to,
perhaps, by the incredible spark-to-tinder response his book
produced in the pews. Robinson has been criticized for fog-
giness, as noted, and Casserley charged he had "befuddled the
minds of men both inside and outside the church to a quite
unprecedented degree." But there was one man at least for
whom the bishop's meaning seemed perfectly clear. And that
was Thomas J. J. Altizer.

In a talk I had with him, Altizer had no difficulty whatever
in assessing the bishop—as an opponent. He identified Robinson as one who was trying desperately to salvage the core of
traditional Christian theology, which Altizer rejected. It was
rather astonishing to find the bishop emerging, from one point
of view, as a kind of Red Cross Knight and defender of the
faith. To mix the metaphor, and possibly to strain it, he might
be described as a man trying to jettison excess cargo from an
aircraft which was dropping perilously close to those peaks
identified on theological charts as Altizer and Hamilton, Nietzsche and Sartre.

From another point of view, however, it might be said that
Robinson opened the door—and Altizer slipped in.

10 The Death of God

Thomas J. J. Altizer, the Young Turk of Christian theology, had gee-whizzed to fame on the strength of a single four-letter word. He was holding on to that word for dear life. And then, for one breathless moment, it appeared as if he might let it dribble through his fingers.

The word was "dead." As in "God is Dead."

The occasion was a symposium at Northwestern University, in the Chicago suburb of Evanston, where Altizer appeared on a panel with Walter Kaufmann, the Princeton philosopher, and Harvey Cox, author of *The Secular City*. Altizer had become the most controversial spokesman for the ultra-radical Death of God theology. Again, this was in 1966, shortly before my meeting with Bishop Robinson at Wabash, and I attended the symposium in hopes of discovering just what it was that Altizer had been trying to say.

Nobody seemed certain. As it developed, nobody had really asked him before. After the symposium I did ask him, and later I had a lengthy interview with him following his return to Atlanta and his duties as associate professor of Bible and religion at Emory University. If nothing else, Altizer made it perfectly clear exactly what he meant.

He arrived at the Northwestern symposium in a canary-yellow sport coat, black slacks, ice-blue shirt, flame-red tie, baby-blue wool socks, and brown brogans. He had tousled black hair and looked a little like the movie actor Glenn Ford. When he addressed the audience, however, he no longer looked like Glenn Ford. He looked and sounded like one of Plato's divine madmen. He had charisma, and lots of it. And what he said was pure poetry. Everybody agreed it was poetry, because it was very beautiful, and nobody could understand it.

"I apologize for my presence," he said. "I'm incapable of speaking about man. I find myself almost speechless. Almost the only word that may be spoken about man in our time is a word that attempts to express the darkness of ourselves. And this darkness is the body of the dead God. . . . If faith can but whisper in our world, it can take a step toward life. And we can never take that step until we truly know that God is Dead. We can say with thanksgiving, 'God is Dead. Thank God.' "

It was not only what Altizer said; it was his tremulous, Margaret O'Brien way of saying it. A professor winced, turned and whispered, "How can he bear to do it—strip himself naked this way?" "He's sick," said one. "Inspired," said another.

Altizer had been described as speaking at times in mystical overtones, but that did not go far enough. Rather, he presented the image of a full-fledged, card-carrying visionary—a profane mystic haunted by an apocalyptic vision of cosmic dimensions. At one point, responding to a sharply worded question, he told the audience in Billy Budd-ish frustration: "Sometimes I feel like a man who stutters and can't speak. Sometimes I feel like a man in a room where a foreign and untranslatable language is being spoken—but he has to speak nevertheless."

As he did speak, his references to the dead God became even more enigmatic. They were voiced in the present and future tenses. "God is." "God will." As it turned out later, this was significant.

Before the audience, Altizer did tend to express himself in arcane symbolism. But later, at a student bull session, a different Altizer took the floor. This was Altizer the scholar, Altizer the theologian, Altizer the metaphysician. The vision was switched off, intellect was switched on, and Altizer himself was no longer obscure; he was instead a thoughtful man who was doing his best to express an obscure idea: like a mathematician who has been asked to describe the taste of peppermint. He was friendly, amusing, intelligent, and eager to communicate. He knew what he meant; questioned carefully, he said what he meant—and he did not mean what most people had seemed to think he meant. Listening to him, it appeared increasingly ironic that Altizer had somehow come to be identified with that mainstream phenomenon known as the New Theology, in so far as that refers to the secularization of the church and a this-worldly involvement in social problems; it seemed even more ironic that the New Theology had come to be identified with Altizer. This was a gigantic error, Altizer agreed. Grinning, puffing on a fragrant pipe, he explained his vision.

What it boiled down to was a highly unorthodox interpretation of the Incarnation: of the Word becoming flesh in the person of Jesus Christ. What Altizer was talking about was transcendence, and immanence.

We have said it is possible to conceive of God as both transcendent *and* immanent, and we recalled the analogy to the relationship between Shakespeare and the characters in *The Tempest.* Shakespeare obviously is immanent in his characters, since they owe their existence to him; but he also transcends them, in the sense that they do not exhaust his being: he has a separate existence above and beyond them. Altizer began with a fairly traditional view of God somewhat along these lines, accepting the idea of a transcendent-immanent divinity. And he also accepted the Incarnation as a historic fact: God manifesting himself in the world in the flesh of Jesus.

For years, however, he brooded upon the full significance of this event. He immersed himself in a study of Eastern mysticism, Nietzsche, Hegel, William Blake—and he thought hard about the Incarnation. Then, one day while he was reading, it came to him. It all fell in place.

The Incarnation happened.

So did the Crucifixion.

But not the Resurrection!

This idea is the essence of Altizer's theology. God had incarnated himself in the body of Jesus; but when Jesus died, God did not "jump back up into heaven." He remained in the world. He is in the world now. What God did, said Altizer, was "empty himself of transcendence." He became totally immanent in the universe. He became part of the universe. But he did not, immediately, become all of the universe.

At first he was immanent only in Jesus. Since the death of

Jesus he has continued to embed himself deeper and deeper into the fabric of the universe. No longer transcendent in any sense, he is in the process even now of becoming ever more immanent.

Jesus, to Altizer, was "the original Christ." Christ was that point where God entered the world. And Altizer retains the word Christ to signify the God who remains in the world, becoming more and more a part of it. The word "spirit" might do just as well, said Altizer. But for various reasons he would prefer to "stick with the word Christ."

More often than not, however, Altizer in his conversation spoke neither of Christ nor of spirit. He kept right on speaking of "God." When this was called to his attention, he conceded: "In a certain sense I treat Christ as God. But the word bears an entirely different meaning from the dominant meaning of God. That's why I resist the word God." He resisted it all evening with little success.

Altizer described the movement toward greater immanence as an evolutionary, creative process; it is leading toward a final Christ: an apocalyptic new godhead in which God will be all there is. Altizer spoke of "a new world that will dawn at the end of the old world." He spoke of "a totally new creation—new man, new world, new life." When he speaks of the death of God, said Altizer, he is speaking of the passage from transcendence to immanence. Eventually the new and different godhead will be realized, he said. But even now, before it is realized, man can rejoice in a new sense of freedom.

Man finds himself in darkness, said Altizer. "And this darkness is the body of the dead God." But once the darkness is recognized for what it is, it can be accepted. "Only a rotting body in a tomb," said Altizer. "It can't bind us to it, once we have known it truly as an empty darkness. Then, at that moment, we can truly be liberated from it." The transcendent power has ended, and man is free.

Shakespeare has entered his own play, Altizer seemed to be saying. Eventually he will be the play—and then he will write a final act which incorporates the preceding five but is wholly different.

"I make the Incarnation everything," Altizer summed up, adding, necessarily, that he gives the rest of the Bible "only a very limited allegiance." His interpretation of the Incarnation was entirely consistent, he said. "Christ has come, and you hurl him back into heaven. This is a complete betrayal of Christ. Only by seeing God's death in Christ can we be true to Christ."

At the bull session, the Northwestern students fired questions at Altizer, and, as they did so, it was possible to trace many of his concepts back to their sources. A wholly immanent God, after all, is scarcely a new idea: it is the idea of Eastern pantheism, pure and simple, and Altizer conceded he was talking pantheism. The God of the East is "very real," he said, and "infinitely more realistic" than the traditional Western God. One could opt for this God, he said. But there is one important sense in which Altizer would distinguish his position from the Eastern view, and we shall return to this point in a later chapter. Briefly, for now, Altizer's theology suggests that the cosmic process is evolutionary—that it is leading up to something—while Eastern metaphysics supposedly rejects the evolutionary hypothesis. The East "looks backward to a primordial totality" (according to Altizer), and Altizer on the other hand "looks forward" to an eschatological totality which is utterly transformed and aware of itself.

Altizer of course had taken his God-is-Dead tag from

160

Nietzsche, and the new sense of freedom echoed Blake's mystical emphasis upon man: his delight in man's liberty and his rejection of any transcendent authority, his absorption with Jesus and his denial of God.

Altizer acknowledged his debt to Blake and Nietzsche.

There also seemed nothing new in the idea of an evolving spirit. That derived from Hegel, as Altizer was pleased to point out. But it also sounded very much like Henri Bergson's vital force. As a matter of fact, it sounded even more like Teilhard de Chardin's view of the universe. Again, we shall have more to say about this in another chapter, and we shall limit ourselves for the moment to only one aspect of Teilhard's metaphysics.

Teilhard, a Jesuit paleontologist, had proposed an evolutionary theory based upon the increasing complexification of inert matter. He proposed that mankind was moving toward the realization of a new godhead which Teilhard referred to as the Omega point. And he saw in this process the hand of God.

The key to it all: the Incarnation.

Teilhard described evolution as "a prodigious biological operation—that of the Redeeming Incarnation." He added: "As early as in St. Paul and St. John we read that to create, to fulfill and to purify the world is, for God, to unify it by uniting it organically with himself."

And how would God unify the world? Teilhard answered: "By partially immersing himself in things, by becoming 'element,' and then, from this point of vantage in the heart of matter, assuming the control and leadership of what we now call evolution." This immersion, said Teilhard, was through Christ—who "put himself in the position (maintained ever since) to subdue under himself . . . the general ascent of consciousness into which he inserted himself. . . . And when he has gathered everything together and transformed everything, he will close in upon himself and his conquests, thereby rejoining, in a final gesture, the divine focus he has never left. Then, as St. Paul tells us, God shall be all in all."

I asked Altizer about this, and Altizer acknowledged his IOU to Teilhard. (He suggested later that I may have overwritten the amount a bit, but I doubt it.) He largely accepted Teilhard's view, Altizer said. It represented "the most important theological work in a long time."

That seemed to leave Altizer with little to call his own, apart from his unique view of the Incarnation. Even there, he appeared to be separated from Teilhard by a single word: *"partially."*

The students jumped on what was left.

"That which was God," said Altizer, "will finally be real and present again in a wholly new form—if you like, in Teilhard's Omega point."

Well, then, God wasn't really dead, was he? Altizer more or less conceded than "transformed" might be more accurate—that the passage from transcendence to immanence meant "a totally new form of the godhead."

"So we shouldn't panic?" asked a student.

"Well," said Altizer, "the Christian church should. Because I'm saying that everything they stand for is dead." Pressed again on his word choice, Altizer said of God: "I think he's dead in a very crucial way . . . in his original divine form. Everything the Christian has called God is dead." All this sounded remarkably close to the minimal concession that theologians had been trying to wring from Altizer for some time. God lives, but man's concept of him is outdated. In my subsequent interview with him, after his return to Georgia, Altizer picked up his word and ran with it again: a less drastic word might fail to make the point, he said—and, as a newspaperman, I could certainly appreciate this. Suppose that first story coming out of Atlanta had begun: "A theologian here says God is immanent." The story would never have come out of Atlanta in the first place; the complex and productive arguments behind the catchword might never have seen the light, and Altizer, at best, would be an obscure Dixie heretic.

The word was not important really. What seemed to upset the Northwestern students far more was Altizer's fundamentally apocalyptic view of the world. Once understood, Altizer appeared to stand in direct contradiction to the radical theology his name had come to dominate—because the main thrust of that theology had probably been messianic and pragmatic.

Radical theology is a big tent, and it has sheltered other theologians who also have said that God is Dead. But these others have not meant that God is Dead in Altizer's sense—nor indeed have they really meant that God is Dead in any sense. Some of the people who are associated with this phrase have meant to say simply that the *word* God is dead; they have abandoned the word as a semantic wreck which means all things to all men, and they have tried to clarify the concept through linguistic analysis. Others have studied God talk as a *cultural* phenomenon, asserting that man creates God in his own image, so to speak—that his idea of God is molded by his cultural prejudices—and they have tried to identify the real divinity which exists perhaps behind the man-made idols. Still others have meant that God is *hidden* or mysterious, as Job found him to be, beyond the power of human comprehension, and they have called upon us to abandon the vain effort to understand God metaphysically, recommending instead that we do God's work by seeking social justice here on earth.

Still another school appears to derive its inspiration largely from Bonhoeffer. Its advocates speak of God as *absent,* in the sense that modern man no longer is capable of experiencing God: the reality of God has somehow gone dead on him. But absence is not the same as death, and Altizer's fellow radical William Hamilton, for example, has referred to "our waiting for God," implying that God perhaps will one day return: it may be that he has simply withdrawn for a time, in order that we may achieve our adulthood in Bonhoeffer's "world come of age." In one of his essays, Hamilton said he followed Bonhoeffer in rejecting *religion*—which is to say, "any system of thought or action in which God or the gods serve as fulfiller of needs or solver of problems." Hamilton described radical theology as a movement from the church to the world—a letting go of God's hand, as it were. And he added: "This combination of a certain kind of God-rejection with a certain kind of world-affirmation is the point where I join the death of God movement. . . . If God is not needed, if it is to the world and not God that we repair for our needs and problems, then perhaps we may come to see that he is to be enjoyed and delighted in. . . . Our waiting for God, our godlessness, is partly a search for a language and a style by which we might be enabled to stand before him once again, delighting in his presence." In other words, we won't come home again until we have made it all by ourselves in the big city, or rather the big cosmos—and then won't Father be proud of us? Then we can sit on the front-porch swing together and trade stories, man to man, and really get to know each other. No more of this writing home for money; enough of this juvenile dependency relationship: Andy Hardy is growing up. We are falling into parody here, but it is not our intention to poke fun; we are merely trying to communicate a rather difficult idea, somewhat in the manner of an editorial-page cartoonist. Hamilton, in any case, has probably been the best-known Death of God theologian next to Altizer, and Hamilton clearly has not been saying the same thing that Altizer has been saying.

Altizer really stands by himself. Only he has taken a position which might be construed to imply an actual Death of God, and even in his case a stretch of the imagination is required to justify that word Death. He is in fact talking about the Transformation of God. Nevertheless, Altizer has been the only Death of God theologian to propose a really radical metaphysics. He has been the only one to suggest that an actual *change* has occurred in the nature or ontology of God. The orthodox atheist says that God never existed in the first place. Bishop Robinson and the demythologizers say we ought to change our ideas about God. Altizer alone says that God himself has changed.

Altizer also rejects the idea that theology has anything to do with social action. In fact he scoffs at the idea, and he ridicules the secularizers who are trying to make the church "relevant." ("Suddenly the church had something to do.") He is not against good works, of course; but he feels that the secularizers are simply putting old wine into new bottles, and Altizer wants a new wine. He can argue, and does, that good works have nothing to do with the relevance of the church; he can argue, and does, that the business of theologians is theology; he can argue, and does, that only he and a few others have been doing theology. Harvey Cox is a physician, Altizer is a metaphysician. Only Altizer has been asking ultimate questions about the nature of God and reality.

The secularizers have been responding to history and to social forces, and many people, missing his meaning, have supposed that Altizer is doing the same thing. They interpret his message as a kind of existential reaction to the modern world and the impact of technology; they think he is this-worldly, as the secularizers are. But that is wrong. Altizer did not start with the world, he said. He started with his vision. That is what he is talking about, and that is what concerns him: not the world as such, but a vision of the world.

Altizer at Northwestern fulminated against otherworldliness. He implied he was this-worldly, since after all he had equated God with this world. It seemed fair, however, to put him in his own category and describe him instead as inner-worldly.

He told the Northwestern students that civil rights was a "phony nineteenth-century issue" as far as church relevance was concerned. In fact, he said, since divine authority had collapsed (since the transcendent deity was dead), there was absolutely no basis left for moral decision-making. "A Christian can't make decisions on Viet Nam," he said. Nor had a Christian much to hope for at the moment. There was, said Altizer, no messianic hope for "this world, this history, this society." There was only the apocalyptic hope for "the total transformation of all things."

"Suppose I accept your dead God?" said a co-ed. "Where do I get my Brownie points?"

Altizer could offer her only Omega points—and a sense of freedom to do something or other. Whatever she wanted to, apparently. He did not offer the God-is-love message of Bishop Robinson and the secularizers. In several hours, in fact, the word love never came up. Just that other word.

Altizer returned to Atlanta, and we later had the following conversation:

Q. Let me see if I understand your viewpoint correctly, from what you said the other night. You believe, do you not, that there once was a transcendent God?

A. Yes.

Q. Was this God wholly transcendent, or was he also immanent in the world?

A. Both transcendent and immanent.

Q. Did he create the world?

A. This gets more difficult theologically. I do not believe in a literal creation or creation story. Frankly, I haven't worked this out. It's merely tentative. But I think in terms of a kind of evolution of the cosmos. There was an original totality in which all things were one—no separation between nature, man, and God. And out of this totality there evolved the world or the cosmos as a distinct entity—and also God. I think in a certain sense God appears as creator in conjunction with the world's coming to exist apart from God.

Q. As I understand it, you believe God emptied himself of transcendence and became immanent in the world—that he incarnated himself in the person of Jesus. That sounds orthodox, to a point. But you stop with the Incarnation. You reject the Resurrection. You say, "God did not jump back up into heaven." You say he stayed right here in the world after the Crucifixion. Is that correct?

A. Correct. I believe the fullness, the totality of God passed into Christ, moving ever more deeply and fully and comprehensively into the world, flesh, consciousness, and experience.

Q. Why did God decide to do this?

167

A. He didn't decide. I understand the Incarnation as implicit and essential in the whole process of cosmic movement. There was no arbitrary point where a decision was reached.

Q. So God is no longer transcendent but is immanent right now in the world?

A. That's right. . . .

Q. But in what is he immanent? In mankind?

A. I wouldn't say only mankind. As I told you at Northwestern, I reverence Teilhard's vision and largely accept it.

Q. By that, I take it you mean God is immanent in the cosmos as a whole?

A. Really yes, in the entire cosmos.

Q. You speak of Jesus as the original Christ. Do you mean by that there have been other, latter-day Christs?

A. Originally the Incarnation was in the man Jesus. And then, following the Crucifixion, Christ progressively enters the fullness of history and experience, ever more fully and comprehensively becoming actual in the world . . . a forward movement . . . Christ becoming ever more actual, ever more real, ever more incarnate.

Q. You mean this is an evolutionary process that isn't finished yet?

A. I like to think of this immanence itself as a gradual process. God once was real and actual as a transcendent lord. He negated himself. Nevertheless, his epiphany or manifestation as lord continues to linger in human experience, and it has a certain reality in that experience. I call this the dead body of God. It's real in human experience. And it will continue to be real until it is totally negated by the total dawning of the incarnate Christ.

Q. You mean there are parts of the cosmos in which Christ is not yet wholly incarnate?

A. Yes.

Q. All this sounds rather like pantheism. Is it?

A. I think it is . . . in the same sense that Teilhard's vision is. In the cosmic process, it's a kind of dynamic pantheism— God ever becoming other than he was in the past—but nevertheless pantheism in that God eventually will be all in all. Call it a dynamic-process pantheism.

Q. Could your immanent God in any sense be interpreted to mean the Holy Ghost?

A. Possibly. I'd almost be willing to use the word spirit. I'd be willing. In part I do. It's just that this word spirit is so kicked around these days. I'd rather stick with the word Christ.

Q. But doesn't all this say something entirely different from God is dead? You keep speaking of God in the present tense and the future tense. You agreed at Northwestern, I believe, that transformed— completely transformed—was perhaps more accurate than dead. That it was the church's concept of God that was utterly dead. Isn't that what you said at Northwestern?

A. Well, I also want to say the transcendent lord is dead. He's become totally immanent, totally flesh, totally world. If I just speak of transformation, I fear the whole point will be lost. I'm really saying that the God a Christian prays to and worships is dead.

Q. Dead? You start with a transcendent God and you end up with an immanent God. It seems to me you've killed the adjective, not the noun. The noun is God, and the noun remains.

A. Yes. All right. But it doesn't remain in the sense that

169

it still is what it was before. That which God has become is wholly other. And there is, to my knowledge, no form of Christian doctrine that admits or asserts this—that God has decisively transformed himself. I think God as God has died, and God has passed into Christ. And he lives in Christ . . . but only lives in Christ himself. If you like, God the father is dead.

Q. Would you call yourself an atheist?

A. Yes. I do.

Q. The question arises, how do you know all this? I believe you have stated that it came to you one day while you were reading in the University of Chicago library. Could you describe the nature of your experience?

A. That must be about ten years ago now. It was the summer of 1955, I guess. I was reading Erich Heller's essay on Nietzsche and Rilke. It was a very intense personal experience. I'd been thinking about these things for years, of course. Suddenly I was overwhelmed. . . . I felt it. I sensed it. And once having sensed it, I've never been able to lose that sense.

Q. I assume this wasn't something you arrived at by a purely rational process, from empirical evidence. Would it be fair to call it a revelation?

A. I'm afraid that would mislead too many people. I think this theological position is simply a consistent consequence of thinking fully and radically about the meaning of the Incarnation. Once you grant that God fully and finally became man in Jesus Christ, you can largely think through this whole thing. Also, it's rooted in what I believe to be modern and contemporary Christian experience and thinking. And I employ people like Blake and Nietzsche as spokesmen for this radical Christian vision. I base my work on theirs.

170

Q. You often speak of your vision. Wasn't this really a personal vision you had?

A. Let's put it this way. I believe there does in fact exist a great body of materials of various kinds that reflect and embody a modern radical Christian vision. For example, the works of William Blake. I haven't had these visions. I'm no visionary. I seek to be an interpreter of them. Then there's also Hegel's logic as a conceptual expression of the same thing. You can build on the vision and think it through. Hegel allows you to see how Blake's vision is really a consistent resolution of the Christian faith.

Q. But you didn't start with Hegel. Wouldn't you say this understanding of yours came originally from a non-rational source?

A. Oh yes. Every kind of understanding comes originally from a source other than the empirical, the rational. I'd include Freud and Marx in that category.

Q. Would it be fair, then, to describe your vision as basically mystical in nature?

A. There is a higher vision; or, if you like, a radically profane mystical vision. There is such a thing as a modern mystical vision, yes. But it's not the same as traditional [otherworldly] mysticism. It's radically profane. It's directed to the here and now—to life, flesh, energy.

Q. You told the students the other night you couldn't help them make up their minds on Viet Nam and other issues. You said your view provided no basis for moral decision-making. What did you mean?

A. Well, basically this. My view does not lead to an ethical system or set of moral laws. I don't think anyone can think

171

responsibly about ethical problems today. Man has lost the ability.

Q. You said civil rights was a phony nineteenth-century issue. What did you mean by that?

A. The problem itself, it seems to me, is basically a matter of a group of people, Negroes, entering bourgeois, middle-class society. And that basically is an eighteenth- or nineteenth-century problem. It's an old problem, not a problem peculiar to the twentieth century. I think the church has falsely prided itself on being able to speak relevantly on this issue, when it's not really a contemporary issue at all. Further, we are now moving into a phase of the problem that's highly technical and modern. And as we do, the church will have increasingly less and less to say. It will have to be solved by technicians basically—by economists and sociologists.

Q. You mean the church shouldn't speak out on the issue?

A. No, that's not the point. The church should not pride itself on being relevant. These church people congratulate themselves. They say, "See how relevant the church is." And I think that's a great illusion.

Q. Are you saying there's no teleological or ultimate basis for any kind of a morality at all?

A. All I'm saying is, as far as I can see right now, there is no source of moral or human insight into contemporary human and social problems. This is a period of terrible darkness we're going through. Either there is no basis for morality or I just can't see it. Nobody else can see it either. But I think it will come. I hope it will.

Q. Shouldn't clergymen involve themselves in civil rights marches?

A. Oh sure, sure. But we've reached the point already where

172

there aren't going to be any civil rights marches. There won't be any role for churchmen to play. Their basic job was to identify the problem, to attract public attention. And now they've done that.

Q. And now they have another job?

A. That's the great problem. What is that job? I think the church has to be totally reformed.

Q. Until you came along, the mainstream of Christian upheaval seemed partly at least a reaction to social forces—Bonhoeffer reacting to the Nazis, Cox to urbanization, Robinson to secularization. The reformers seemed to be calling for social involvement and more or less suspending judgment on the fine points of theology. That is, they seemed to start with the world. But you seem to start with this inner vision of yours. Is that a fair statement?

A. Yes. It's fair to say I started with the vision rather than the world.

Q. And your vision should in no way be interpreted as a call to social action, to solve the problems of the world?

A. That's right. That's not for me. But I don't want to say it can't involve social action. Each one must find his own way. It's a new kind of freedom if you like. This is why the Death of God is pretty crucial. There's no longer any kind of divine law to follow. It's no longer there.

Q. How would you differentiate yourself from people like Harvey Cox and Bishop Robinson, who say Christians should seek God by involving themselves directly in the problems of the world?

A. The people I call secularists, they're basically church reformers. They're reacting to a form of Christian religiosity which has turned itself completely away from our world. They

173

want basically to restructure the form of the church, to make the church relevant. They're not concerned with transforming the heart of the Christian gospel. They think that's the same, and that's given, always. I myself, and Hamilton and others, belong to a radical group who believe the very heart of the Christian center has got to be transformed. The transcendent God the church has worshiped is no more. One difference is, Cox is not really a theologian. He's not interested in constructing a theological vision or system. Robinson, too. I'm concerned with a full theological understanding of contemporary faith.

Q. In other words, you're more metaphysical?

A. Yes. Except that word is such a . . . it makes people see red. I'm not a Thomist or anything like that. But I am concerned with an ultimate vision, with a full understanding of faith in the world today. Teilhard was metaphysical in this sense.

Q. As one of the students asked the other night, "Where do I get my Brownie points?" What good does your vision do, and what's in it for me? Isn't it just morbid introspection, this naming of the darkness?

A. I think it's liberating to know God is Dead. Otherwise, inevitably, consciously or unconsciously, we will look upon reality as being something alien. Something we can't really know. We'll be victims of it, slaves of it, because it's mysterious. To know God is Dead is to be liberated from the threat of an unknown world, the threat of mystery.

Q. What is the nature of the light you say you see burning beyond the darkness?

A. That dawns in accordance with the degree with which darkness is unveiled. And it's a light that makes possible freedom from oppression right now. To the extent that we're lib-

174

erated from darkness, we are able to give ourselves to life. And life itself becomes light. Darkness becomes light.

Q. This ultimate consummation we're moving toward—is the nature of it predestined? Or is the evolutionary process creative, in the Bergsonian sense?

A. Something like the latter. Except that everything that happens in the world will be a part of that final Omega point.

Q. You said the other night that God in a certain sense remains transcendent. What did you mean?

A. We were speaking in the context of Judaism. I think the Jew can indeed know a transcendent God. The Jew lives in a kind of eternal covenant with God, and he can preserve this because he lives in exile—because he is not totally involved in our history.

Q. How can this be? Are you saying there are two Gods, a Jewish God who's alive and a Christian God who's Dead?

A. The Jew actually is in communion with that ancient epiphany of God—has preserved and perpetuated that moment in faith.

Q. But you said that was over. Are you saying Jews worship a God who isn't there—a false God?

A. It's a false God as far as the Christian is concerned. But I see no reason for the Christian to attack it as such. What must be attacked are the forms of Judaism that maintain themselves within Christianity. That's the real danger.

Q. But is it a false God as far as the Jew is concerned? Are you simply saying the Jew has a right to worship as he pleases?

A. No. I think It's possible for the Jew actually to be in communion with this God. Christians must be totally immersed in history. Jews don't have to be. They're in exile.

Q. I think there was another sense in which you said God

175

remains transcendent. You were debating the point with a philosophy major, and finally you agreed with him.

A. Oh! The problem there was, he was using transcendent in a different sense—to refer to something beyond the given, beyond the brute actuality of experience. He was using it in terms of vision. That's in a sense transcendent. In that sense, everything I say is transcendental.

Altizer said he represents a far more basic challenge to orthodox Christianity than the secularizers do, and no doubt he does —for he represents that influx of Eastern ideas we talked about: he represents pantheism. And pantheism is in the air, no question about that. The doctrine of transcendence is challenged today as never before, and in Altizer's theology—as in LSD cultism—Eastern immanence is given full and final expression. In one of his articles, Altizer called upon the American theologian to "cast off his German tutors" and "open himself both to the religious world of the East and to the deeper sensibility of the Western present." He added: "From the East we may once more learn the meaning of the sacred. . . . We can encounter in the East a form of the sacred which Christianity has never known, a form which is increasingly showing itself to be relevant to our situation."

Obviously, the leap to the East is just as evident in radical theology as it is in the drug movement, at least in so far as this implies a leap from transcendence to immanence—and if Altizer has been the only important theologian so far to embrace pantheism without reservation, less radical radicals have been embracing it with reservations. On a superficial level at least, it is not much of a jump from Robinson's position to Altizer's (which is not to imply that Altizer derives from Robinson; in fact, Altizer was publishing his views for a non-popular readership several years before *Honest to God* saw print), and radical theology on the whole can be characterized essentially as a movement in the direction of immanence. It is significant perhaps that Harvey Cox, that squarest of all the radicals, was able to defend transcendence at Northwestern only in a very limited way. He suggested it was "too early" to foreclose the possibility of a transcendent God; the discussion, he said, should "remain open." It could be that man is simply incapable of answering the question one way or the other.

Once the shock effect has worn off, the Death of God slogan may lose much of its appeal, and Altizer perhaps will suffer an eclipse. Once understood, his apocalyptic message is not likely to capture the imagination of this messianic Peace Corps generation, and his unique view of the Incarnation is subject to considerable criticism. To some degree at least, Altizer has owed his success to the fact that few people have actually grasped his meaning—the attacks against him have not been well informed—and, from one point of view, the best way to attack him is to explain him fully. But the loss of an unfortunate slogan will not put an end to the radical examination of transcendence, and Altizer's path to immanence is not the only one.

Altizer is both in and out of the radical mainstream. He is in it so far as he leans toward immanence; he is out of it so far as he rejects the messianic hope for this world in the here and now. Particularly is he out of it in his apparent rejection (or neglect) of a primary essence or condition of Being which might provide the basis for an ethical system. This essence or condition has meanwhile been given its due by the drug movement and by the bishop of Woolwich—and it also is central to that emerging phenomenon which is sometimes described as humanistic psychology.

11 Humanistic psychology

It is said that Freud had an almost pathologic fear of meta-physics. According to Jung, Freud was appalled by the "occult" implications he encountered in his exploration of the human psyche. Probing ever deeper into the mysteries of the uncon-scious region, he heard whispers perhaps from that unseen world William James talked about—and they frightened him.

Freud confessed to him, said Jung, "that it was necessary to make a dogma of his sexual theory because this was the sole bulwark of reason against a possible 'outburst of the black flood of occultism.'" Consider, for example, the idea of intra-uterine memories, or recollections of life in the womb. If carried further this might suggest the possibility at least of pre-uterine memories —which in turn might lend some support to the Eastern doc-trine of reincarnation. Freud refused to consider such implications, and this necessarily resulted in his negative attitude toward the unconscious, which he regarded as a sort of garbage heap for man's brute instincts. As a consequence, said Jung, psychology became for the most part "the science of conscious contents, measured as far as possible by collective standards." But suppose for a moment that the unconscious is something more than this. What if it is in fact man's link to ultimate reality and the Ground of his Being?

Psychology has finally started to consider this possibility, urged on in part by psychedelic evidence. In a pioneering study, humanistic psychologist Abraham H. Maslow proposed that his fellow psychologists move *Toward a Psychology of Being,* and Maslow's unorthodox theories have recently inspired something of a Freud is Dead movement. The development is comparable in many ways to the radical upheaval in theology, and Maslow might well be described as the Bonhoeffer or Robinson of psychology.

What does this mean, a psychology of Being?

Maslow began by agreeing in a sense with Robinson and disagreeing with Sartre. He began with the assertion that every man has *"an essential biologically based inner nature."* This inner nature "is to some degree 'natural,' intrinsic, given, and, in a certain limited sense, unchangeable, or, at least, unchanging." (That is to say, it is unconditional—from Robinson's viewpoint, transcendent.) Moreover, it is not bad or evil: it is either neutral in character or positively good. Man therefore would do well to discover and develop it; rather than suppress it, he should follow it: he should live his life according to its dictates. Psychology likewise should acknowledge it and seek to understand it.

Freudian psychology is preoccupied with pathology; it is

primarily a sick psychology, or a psychology of sickness. But it fails to define health. Or rather it tends simply to equate healthy behavior with successful adjustment to the social environment, nothing more, and it regards conscience as a sort of learned response: an internalization of one's "shall" and "shall not" parents. It is situational and subjective. It does not suggest the existence of any values, goals, or ideals in any sense absolute, objective, or unconditional, and it does not provide for the possibility of an ultimate reality or ultimate state of Being.

On the other hand, Being psychology is a psychology of health. It defines healthy behavior in terms of successful adjustment to one's essential inner nature, and it regards conscience as the "unconscious or preconscious" perception of that nature. It affirms, of course, the existence (or potential existence) of an ultimate reality or state of Being, and it says, in effect, "to thine own Self be true." It does not ask what men do: it asks what they should do. It asks what men are, but it also asks what men might be and should become.

Being psychology indicates that man has a built-in potential, as it were, like the oak which is hidden in the acorn, and conscience is the intuitive awareness of that potential. The Freudian superego may also exist, but its demands are imposed from outside: from the society and the culture, transmitted by the parents. The conscience of Being, by comparison, is intrinsic; its demands are imposed from within, by the essential inner nature: it is an inner voice which insists that we be true to that nature, true to the future, true to the truth.

Being psychology, or B-psychology, is different from Deficiency psychology, or D-psychology. D-psychology studies sick people whose basic needs have not been satisfied—who are afflicted, so to speak, with psychic deficiency diseases. B-psychology

studies healthy people whose basic needs have been satisfied—
and who therefore can devote their energies to life, to the world,
and to growth: to the actualization of their essential inner
natures.

Maslow developed his theories in part by studying a class of
healthy people he described variously as meta-motivated, growth-
dominated, and self-actualizing. He also referred to this type
as inner-determined rather than outer-determined, recalling the
sociologist David Riesman's distinction between the inner-di-
rected individualist and the other-directed conformist. He said
further that self-actualizing people appear to be capable of a
special kind of love and a special kind of cognition. These he
termed B-love and B-cognition, as opposed to D-love and D-
cognition, the letters again standing for Being on the one hand
and Deficiency on the other. What is more, he said, a capacity
for B-love and B-cognition will sometimes enable a self-actu-
alizer to achieve a special kind of experience—an intense, if
fleeting, moment of utter joy and complete fulfillment. This
Maslow called a "peak experience."

D-love is a selfish love in which the lover seeks primarily to
satisfy his own needs; in short, it is I-It love. B-love is un-
selfish, non-possessive admiration for the Being of another person; in short, it is I-Thou love. Similarly, D-cognition can be
summed up here as the I-It mode of perception and understanding, while B-cognition refers to an I-Thou view of the
world.

In B-cognition during a peak experience, said Maslow, an
object is not perceived in terms of use, purpose, or relation to
anything else; it is perceived as a whole. "It is seen as if it were
all there was in the universe, as if it were all of Being, synonymous with the universe." The B-cognizer becomes totally ab-

sorbed with the object to the exclusion of all else, and he admires it without comparing it, evaluating it, judging it, or desiring to possess it; above all, he does not *rubricize* the object, which means to say he does not attempt to classify it or put it in a category with other objects. The B-cognizer, moreover, is relatively "ego-transcending, self-forgetful, ego-less." He also is non-motivated in terms of future action; he regards the peak experience as a "self-validating" end in itself and not as the means to some future end. A "very characteristic disorientation to time and space" occurs, and the B-cognizer finds himself, subjectively, outside of time and space. He is "most here-now, most free of the past and of the future." He is therefore "non-striving, non-needing, non-wishing." His perception is non-dualistic, and he thus denies the existence of evil—or views it rather as "only a partial phenomenon, a product of not seeing the world whole and unified." Being as such is good, or neutral. And finally, the peak experience is beyond abstractions—including verbal abstractions. It cannot really be put into words, since it is after all a view of the whole, and words cannot express the whole.

B-psychology's description of a healthy person's peak experience sounds very much, of course, like James's description of mystical religious experience, Buber's description of I-Thou experience, the drug cultist's description of psychedelic experience, and the Zen Buddhist's description of *satori*. Maslow's essential inner nature, as we have already indicated, sounds very much like Tillich's Ground of Being and Bishop Robinson's transcendent or unconditional God. And the B-psychologist's attitude toward the unconscious would certainly appear to support the view of James and Jung. "Because the roots of ill health were found first in the unconscious," wrote Maslow, "it has been

182

our tendency to think of the unconscious as bad, evil, crazy, dirty or dangerous, and to think of the primary processes as *distorting* the truth. But now that we have found these depths to be also the source of creativeness, of art, of love, of humor and play, and even of certain kinds of truth and knowledge, we can begin to speak of a healthy unconscious, of healthy regressions. . . . We can now go into primary process cognitions for certain kinds of knowledge, not only about the self but also about the world."

Maslow, unlike Robinson, did not attempt to say in so many words what man's essential inner nature might be. But a clue to his thought is provided perhaps by his expression of wonder at "the mystery of communication between alone-nesses via, e.g., intuition and empathy, love and altruism, identification with others, and homonomy in general." Maslow added: "We take these for granted. It would be better if we regarded them as miracles to be explained."

The scientist Lecomte du Noüy expressed the same idea in his book *Human Destiny* when he pointed out that "the appearance of moral and spiritual ideas remains an absolute mystery." How, then, are we to account for our "unaccountable aspirations"? The scientific unbeliever insists upon cause and effect —and then refuses to acknowledge any cause creating such effects as love, conscience, charity, and sacrifice. The cause is denied because it cannot be seen. Thus, as physicist David Bohm has noted, nineteenth-century positivists such as Mach held that the idea of atoms was meaningless and "nonsensical" because atoms could not then be observed. But even science will sometimes accept the evidence of things not seen, as in the case of the outer planets. The existence of some unseen planet was first suspected because of perturbations in the orbit of Uranus;

183

when a proper telescope was brought to bear, giant Neptune swam into view—and Pluto later was similarly discovered. So what would happen if we were to focus our attention on the phenomena of love and morality, searching in the same way for the source of these perturbations? What might swim into view in this case?

Evidence of an essential inner nature led Maslow to reconsider the possibility that mankind might be able to develop a humanistic morality or scientific ethic. As it is, Western morality tends to be legalistic and authoritarian; our basic rules of conduct are handed down from above, as it were, in the form of commandments, on tablets of stone, and we are expected to obey them without asking questions. Thou shalt not kill, for example. No doubt that is a very good law, and there is probably a very good reason for it—but we are not told what the reason is. Similarly, no particular reason is given for the less basic rules of conduct which are imposed upon us by mundane authority. As a general proposition, all in all, we are expected to behave this way or that way because God said so, or our parents said so, or Congress said so, or Emily Post said so.

The system does work, in a fashion, if we sense that the laws in question are for some reason good ones. Thus most of us feel intuitively that the law against killing is a good law, which explains why it has remained on the books for so many years in so many lands, and most of us therefore do not kill other people, unless of course we are told to by Congress or the President. But the system breaks down too, and especially so in an age of empiricism when people develop the disturbing habit of demanding a reason for everything. We are distressed, for example, when criminals and juvenile delinquents band together in gangs, make their own rules, and refuse to honor the laws of

society. We wonder why it happens. But society itself is a gang
—it is simply a very big gang—and its rules are no more sacro-
sanct than the Mafia's unless some valid reason can be produced
to recommend them: a reason, preferably, which will demonstrate that the rules as such are grounded in the very nature of
things. This is why men have dreamed of discovering a "natural
law" which is grounded in the nature of Being itself, demon-
strably true and irrefutable: a law which no man could possibly
deny, having once understood it.

Such a law indeed is central to the Tibetan concept of
Dharmakaya. As the Evans-Wentz edition of the *Tibetan Book
of the Dead* tells us: "*Dharmakaya* is the norm of all existence,
the standard of truth, the measure of righteousness, the good
law; it is that in the constitution of things which makes certain
modes of conduct beneficial and certain other modes detrimen-
tal." In the East, for instance, human compassion is a matter of
elementary logic based upon the supposedly monistic character
of mankind. "When you're cut, I bleed. Therefore, I had better
see to it that you are not cut." In the West the idea of a natural
law can be traced back to Plato's assertion that virtue and
knowledge are the same thing: that all real virtue springs from
knowledge alone. Saint Augustine perhaps was hinting at something of this sort when, addressing himself to God, he bemoaned
the crimes of Sodom. "But how can men's insults touch you,
who are undefiled? Or what injury can be committed against
you, who cannot be hurt? But your vengeance is in that which
men do against themselves, because when they sin against you,
they are acting wickedly against their own souls, and *iniquity
gives itself the lie*." Robinson likewise in his New Morality was
attempting to establish an ethic based on love, the Ground of
Being, and he believed that this could be accomplished by de-

mythologizing the legalistic Christian ethic. The West of course insists that the character of mankind is pluralistic and personal, not monistic and impersonal; in East and West alike, however, those who affirm the existence of a natural law are in fundamental agreement on one point: they all base their arguments on the existence of a primary state of Being. Natural morality is not possible unless Sartre was wrong and such a primary state of Being actually exists; it matters not in this case whether you refer to that state as Atman or as an essential inner nature. Here, then, we discover a critical point of convergence which brings together the drug movement, radical theology, B-psychology, and Eastern metaphysics.

Maslow, for his own part, conceded that all past attempts to realize a natural morality had failed. But he added that contemporary developments in psychology "make it possible for us for the first time to feel confident that this age-old hope may be fulfilled if only we work hard enough." If men knew what they really were like, and what they were meant to become, the very nature of their Being would emerge as "a court of ultimate appeal for the determination of good and bad." It would at last become possible to establish a system of "morals-from-within." In the past, all efforts to establish such a system have been frustrated by man's apparent inability to determine what his essential inner nature actually is. It is all very well to say there is a primary state of Being—but how does one form any precise knowledge of it?

Maslow thought he now saw a way to solve this problem. The first step would be for psychology to abandon its exclusive interest in sickness. Let psychology turn its attention *also* to a study of health, and of ends and values as well. Specifically, let it study the habits and attitudes of healthy, self-actualizing people: the growth-dominated B-cognizers and B-lovers who have peak experiences. Maslow said that "it looks as if *there were* a single ultimate value for mankind, a far goal toward which all men strive." All men to some degree are struggling to attain that goal, which is the realization of their essential inner nature; but the self-actualizers by comparison have the goal already in sight. Presumably, then, psychology could learn a good deal by keeping the self-actualizers under close observation—by examining, for example, the hedonic *choices* they make in the course of their daily lives: by taking careful note of the things that delight them. And why do this? Because, said Maslow, such people will automatically make the right choices. They will choose virtue just as we choose a dessert, because virtue delights them. "They spontaneously tend to do right because that is what they *want* to do, what they *need* to do, what they enjoy . . ." To such self-disciplined people, said Maslow, we can safely say: "Do as you will, and it will probably be all right." And if this sounds familiar, it may remind us of that Augustinian directive from which Robinson constructed his New Morality.

Through the self-actualizers, therefore, psychology can discover "which values men trend toward." Indeed, said Maslow, "it is possible that we may soon even *define* therapy as a search for values." This in turn calls to mind a cartoon which appeared in the *New Yorker,* I believe, quite a long time ago. A psychiatrist glares down at the free-associating patient on his couch and snarls, "You cur!" Or something to that effect. The idea seemed funny at the time, but in a sense it is just the sort of attitude Maslow has proposed. Psychology should start making value judgments. It should say: "Here is what it is like to be fully human." "This is wrong." "That is right."

Maslow failed to dispose entirely of one problem: who decides what health is, and who chooses the self-actualizers? If such an all-wise person exists, then why bother with the self-actualizers? Why not study him instead? Again we meet one of those saber-toothed circles, and here again the matter might rest —if Maslow stood alone in the witness box. As we have already indicated, however, the case for a primary state of Being is bolstered by the supporting testimony of psychedelic experience, mystical experience, radical theology, and the Eastern movement as such. Coming together as they do, all of these give added weight to Maslow's argument, just as Maslow's argument gives added weight to them. Also, each of them provides as it were an additional laboratory tool with which to probe the unconscious—and thereby to test the assertions of B-psychology. It is not necessary to depend upon peak experience alone, or any one person's definition of a peak experience. The psychedelics would appear to be especially promising in this connection, and, in so far as it enables men to know themselves better, LSD makes a natural morality far more of a possibility than it has ever been before. There is some evidence that LSD in effect anesthetizes the Freudian superego—puts to sleep those internalized parents —and thus allows the intrinsic conscience to take over.

If you grant the validity of a primary state of Being, what are the practical implications of this? What would a natural morality actually mean in terms of human conduct? The answer is obvious if you assume that the primary state is monistic in character—you're cut, I bleed—and this interpretation in fact suggests a possible distinction between law and justice. If mankind were a single man, and that man had a gangrenous arm, law would simply whack off the arm to save the man. Justice would first do all it could to save the arm. Justice would not be interested in punishing the arm, for the sake of punishment—and while justice itself might consent finally to radical surgery, it would do so only as a last resort. Law recognizes the integrity of the whole. Justice recognizes the integrity of the whole, but it recognizes also the parts' participation in that whole. Monism therefore provides a firm basis for decision-making in interpersonal relationships. It is a question simply of how much you are willing to hurt yourself. Are the gains worth the pains—always remembering that the pains are really yours? (If Stalin had been a monist, for example, he might have hesitated over his decision to liquidate the kulaks.) Indeed, this does seem to be the direction in which our court system is presently moving, to the despair of many good citizens.

As a general observation, in fact, whatever our voiced convictions, it might be said that we *act* as if life were monistic. I am struck by this personally whenever I see a fire engine racing to a fire, or the United Nations in emergency session—whenever society mobilizes its resources in some dramatic fashion to protect the welfare of individuals or the common good. And what, for that matter, is the real meaning of our personal and social gregariousness?

But after all, it is possible to account for such phenomena without resorting to an unqualified monism. While it seeks to preserve the integrity of individual personality, Western religious tradition has been just as insistent that there are bonds which in some ineffable way unite us all. We are told this again now by radical theology, by B-psychology, and especially perhaps by the drug movement. Whether or not mankind is utterly monistic, psychedelic experience does seem to hint at a brotherhood which is something more than brotherhood—and to this extent it may help to provide a rationale for social action, includ-

189

ing civil rights. As the LSD researcher Willis W. Harman has said in connection with those who somehow manage to break the spell of cultural hypnosis, whatever the means, a man who is privileged to look at ultimate reality will know thereafter from his own experience "that we are elements of a greater whole, and that what one does to another he does ineluctably to himself."

A monistic awareness, qualified or not, might also explain why LSD has proved helpful in treating alcoholics, who say they no longer feel isolated from the rest of the world, and in easing the anguish of terminal patients, who have reported new insights into the real meaning of life, death, and immortality.

In so far as it confirms an unconditional human nature, LSD might also be helpful in solving another philosophical problem. Implicit in the idea of a natural ethic based upon a primary state of Being is a possible validation of free will—as opposed to a mechanistic determinism. The modern argument for free will has been founded very often upon the science of quantum physics and Heisenberg's famous Principle of Uncertainty or Indeterminacy. Heisenberg said it is impossible for science to predict the behavior of an individual particle at the atomic level, since the very act of observation and measurement will influence the behavior of the particle. (This has been compared with the difficulty a blind man would encounter if he attempted to learn about a snowflake by touching one.) But some physicists have gone even further; carrying uncertainty to the point of indeterminacy, they have asserted that individual particles actually behave in a chaotic, capricious, and lawless manner. You can never tell what a particular particle is going to do next, and thus there is no causality or determinism in the microcosmos. The laws of nature are derived only when you apply the theory of statistical probability to a vast number of particles; then individual capriciousness will cancel out, and it is possible to predict how matter will behave in the macrocosmos. Flip a coin once and it will come up either heads or tails. Flip it a million times and it will almost certainly come up heads a half-million times and tails a half-million times.

Some philosophers and theologians have seized upon this idea, finding in microcosmic anarchy a possible justification for the thesis that man himself has free will. This of course links free will inexorably to physics, and it is perhaps a rather dangerous position. In the first place, there are those who suggest that the lawlessness of the particles is only apparent; as Bohm has proposed, an explanation for microcosmic behavior may yet be discovered at some deeper level of causation below the atomic and subatomic. And where would that leave free will, if not on a sawed-off limb? More to the point, as philosopher Ernst Cassirer has argued, ethics would surely be in a sorry position if it had to take refuge in the gaps of scientific knowledge—in a mere possibility which is, essentially, negative in nature. Should freedom be equated with causelessness? Is that the kind of ethic you would really prefer if you had your choice? Could you *trust* such an ethic, and could you trust any person whose actions were determined by a capricious whim? Or would you prefer instead an ethic which is grounded in reason, and would you rather do business with somebody whose conduct is determined by his essential inner nature? Describing Spinoza's views on the subject, Cassirer wrote: "To act freely does not mean to act arbitrarily or without prior decision; it means rather to act in accordance with a decision which is in harmony with the essence of our reason. This essence and with it the specific priority of reason consists of the knowledge of the whole." True ethical judgment, said Cassirer, does not put a high value on capricious behavior; rather, "it values a course of action that springs from the basic substratum of the personality and is firmly anchored in it."

Natural morality is predicated of course on just such a substratum—on a primary state of Being—and it suggests in turn a kind of freedom we might describe as *ontological freedom*. This has nothing to do with anarchy or lawlessness. It implies a freedom to be yourself—or more exactly, a freedom to become that which you were meant to be. In this sense, freedom for Beethoven would not mean a freedom to become a sailor or an architect or an outlaw: it would mean simply a freedom to become a composer of music. In the same sense, freedom for the acorn would be a freedom to become an oak tree—not a hibiscus or a sugar maple, but only an oak. Freedom, in other words, means the freedom to realize your essential inner nature, and Beethoven for example would be subject to a blind determinism only if his father, say, forced him to study medicine. Ontological freedom applies both to the individual and to the whole, and it is valid even if the whole should prove to be in fact monistic.

Here too Spinoza has spoken. If we *are* nothing more than parts of a whole which is in the process of realizing itself, we nevertheless contribute to that whole, each and every one of us. It is an expression of us, just as much as we are an expression of it. In so far as we partake of the whole, we each of us determine in part what the whole is and shall be. If we are cogs in a machine, we are not merely the servants of the machine: we each of us in part comprise the machine, and it is just as much subservient to us as we are subservient to it. In fact, we are the machine, and the machine is us. (What was it Bergson said?

192

The universe is a machine for the making of God?) In so far as the whole is free, then we also are free—in so far as we partake of the whole. The sense of a dictatorial determinism arises only when we fail to recognize our true identity or essential inner nature, and it matters not whether that identity is pluralistic or monistic. The sense of freedom arises with our *awareness* of our identity—of our destiny, if you will—and we recognize that we are free when we understand that we are responding either to our own inner nature or to the inner nature of a whole in which we partake. This perhaps is a deeper meaning of the saying "You shall know the truth and the truth shall set you free." The truth is our essential inner nature, pluralistic or otherwise, and, to the extent that it provides us with a greater awareness of the truth, the psychedelic experience sets us free—as do also the peak and mystical experiences. Or so at least the argument might run.

In his important book *The Secular City*, Harvey Cox has asserted that "the era of metaphysics is dead" and that "politics replaces metaphysics as the language of theology." Perhaps metaphysics *is* dead for Cox, who apparently subscribes to the doctrine of God's hiddenness. But obviously it is very much alive for Altizer, for Bishop Robinson, for B-psychology, for the drug cults, for the Eastern movement. In this case Cox may have completely misread the signs of the times, for it appears far more likely that we are witnesses today to a significant rebirth of metaphysics. As we have shown, even psychology is now asking ultimate ontological questions about the nature of Being. And perhaps it was inevitable that psychology should do this. As Tillich has indicated, there are two kinds of anxiety—neurotic and existential—and only ontology can distinguish the one from the other. Neurotic anxiety is unreal, or rather has a misplaced object of attention, while existential anxiety is the result of a realistic analysis of the way things actually are. Clearly it is important to distinguish the two, and that is why Tillich complained about "the lack of an ontological analysis of anxiety and a sharp distinction between existential and pathological anxiety."

Two decades ago, at the end of the war, Jacques Maritain wrote: "What is essentially needed is a renewal of metaphysics. . . . What is needed first and foremost is a rediscovery of Being, and by the same token a rediscovery of love. This means, axiomatically, a rediscovery of God. The existential philosophies which are today in fashion are but a sign of a certain deep want and desire to find again the sense of Being."

He said further: "In perceiving Being Reason knows God."

Those words have a prophetic ring now. A rediscovery of Being is central to the contemporary developments we have discussed, and from one point of view it might be said that man today is making another desperate effort to find his God again. But, as noted, the rediscovered God has seemed more often than not to be the Eastern God, and the new metaphysics has been deeply influenced by mysticism. Today's radical ontology may therefore be subject to a Western-oriented criticism, including a major objection which was expressed some years ago, in another connection, by no one less than Tillich:

"Mysticism," said Tillich, "does not take seriously the concrete and the doubt concerning the concrete. It plunges directly into the ground of being and meaning, and leaves the concrete, the world of finite values and meanings, behind. Therefore it does not solve the problem of meaninglessness. In terms of the present religious situation this means that Eastern mysticism is not the solution of the problems of Western Existentialism, although many people attempt this solution."

194

Buber raised the same point in rejecting the Eastern concept of a mystical union with the godhead: "What does it help my soul that it can be withdrawn anew from this world here into unity, when this world itself has of necessity no part in the unity—what does all 'enjoyment of God' profit a life that is rent in two? If that abundantly rich heavenly moment has nothing to do with my poor earthly moment—what has it then to do with me, who have still to live, in all seriousness still to live, on earth?"

This brings us back to questions we asked earlier. Are the East and the West as diametrically opposed as they appear to be? Or are they both perhaps attempting to say the same thing, in different ways?

12 The Jordan and the Ganges

Nature does not count, said Bergson. Neither does it measure.

The French philosopher, who died in 1941, has been harshly judged for his anti-intellectualism and for the essential role he assigned to intuition in man's perception of ultimate reality. But his views on the limitations of the intellect have acquired a new significance today in light of the contemporary developments we have discussed in this book, and they may help illuminate an important aspect of drug cultism and related movements. In Bergson, indeed, those movements may yet discover their metaphysician.

In criticizing intellect, and therefore science as well, Bergson asserted that intellect has its eyes turned always to the rear. By this he meant that the rational mind is concerned primarily with prediction based on past experience, or in other words with the

196

anticipation that cause-and-effect events will repeat themselves in the future. And intellect favors this kind of perception because intellect is interested only in action, or in using things by acting upon them (I-It). Lecomte du Noüy made the same point, no doubt taking it from Bergson, when he commented, "The aim of science is to foresee, and not, as has often been said, to understand." Of course it *does* foresee. It is highly successful as far as its own limited goals are concerned, and the world's work could not be done without it. But it does *not* understand, and philosophers delude themselves, said Bergson, "when they import into the domain of speculation a method of thinking made for action." Cause-and-effect prediction is valid enough in one sense, but the intellect in another sense has actually created cause and effect. It has done so by artificially dividing and, as it were, freezing in time a reality which in fact consists of a dynamic and indivisible Whole. The intellect cannot comprehend movement, and it cannot comprehend the Whole. In short, it cannot comprehend life.

Dividing? Freezing? What did Bergson mean?

In the first instance, to borrow an example which Bergson used himself, suppose for a moment that reality consisted of a curved line. Science imagines it can grasp the ultimate truth about life by chopping the Whole into pieces—by reducing reality to ever smaller units of matter and energy. Science therefore would divide the curved line into individual points or segments, and it would then try to explain the Whole in terms of its parts. But each of the individual segments would, in itself, be almost a straight line—and the smaller the segment, the greater the illusion of straightness. Thus, by restricting its vision, science quite likely would propose that reality consists of a straight line, or rather a series of straight lines. Following the same sort of logic, we can imagine science announcing the discovery that Wordsworth's ode is composed of twenty-six basic particles (the letters of the alphabet), and while this observation is perfectly correct, it hardly captures the meaning and significance of the poem as a Whole.

As for movement, Bergson likened the intellect to a motion picture camera. The intellect simulates movement by taking a series of snapshots, each one of which is frozen in time for purpose of analysis. Intellect studies these snapshots and thinks that in doing so it is studying true motion. But clearly it is not. This Bergson referred to as the *cinematographical fallacy*, which has its basis in "the absurd proposition that movement is made of immobilities." And thus Bergson explained the paradoxes of the ancient Greek philosopher Zeno, including the paradox of the arrow fired from a point A to a point B. According to Zeno, the flying arrow must successively occupy a series of lesser points between A and B, and it must obviously be at rest at each such point, at least for a moment; therefore it is motionless during the entire course of its passage. Or again, the arrow in its flight must first cover half the distance from A to B. But before it can do that, it must first cover half the distance from A to the midpoint. And half of that distance. And half of *that* distance. And so on, until at last we see that it is impossible for the arrow to get started at all. But we know that the arrow does travel from A to B, so there must be something wrong with Zeno's argument, and Bergson resolved the problem by suggesting that the flight is in fact "an indivisible movement." Once the flight is over, you can count as many imaginary points as you like along its trajectory. The fact remains that the flight itself was accomplished "in one stroke," from A to B, although a certain amount of time was required for this flight. Thus Bergson accused the

198

intellect of neglecting time, or duration, as an actual factor in the mosaic of reality. Science deals with points of time, he said, but it does not deal with time itself or with motion as such.

On the other hand, said Bergson, instinct directly installs itself within movement and reality. It refuses to recognize those points of time and those snapshots of life which are nothing more than "arrests of our attention." Instinct thereby provides us with a form of knowledge which is "practically useless, except to increase pure understanding of reality."

Bergson did not advocate that we rely solely on instinct. Nor did he deny the necessary function of the intellect. But he did reject an utter reliance on intellect alone or instinct alone. The one is necessary for survival, the other for understanding. "There are things that intelligence alone is able to seek, but which, by itself, it will never find. These things instinct alone could find; but it will never seek them." But *intuition* can both seek and find them. Intuition for Bergson was a combination of instinct and intelligence—it was instinct guided by intelligence —and the same happy marriage has been proposed by many others, including Gibran. Thus instinct is the wind which fills the sails of our little ship, as it skims over the waves of this earthly existence. And intellect is the rudder with which we steer the ship. Similarly, life is complicated only when we consider its parts rather than the Whole, and its apparent complexity increases in proportion with the number of parts which we synthetically ascribe to that Whole. And this perhaps is the basis of the Hindu teaching: "He who knows OM knows all." (He who knows the monistic One knows all.) If the consciousness that slumbers in instinct should awake, said Bergson, "it would give up to us the most intimate secrets of life." It would do so by revealing to us the Whole, philosophy being nothing less than man's attempt to dissolve once more into that Whole from which he has estranged himself—that Whole where there are no measurements and no laws (only science has laws, not nature), where "there is nothing left but the reality that flows, together with the knowledge ever renewed that it impresses on us of its present state."

That, in brief, was Bergson's case against a slavish reliance on the rational intellect, and it would seem that his point of view today is reflected to a considerable extent in the assertions of radical theology, psychology, and pharmacology. Maslow, for example, has expressed his criticism of "the need-motivated kind of perception, which *shapes* things . . . in the manner of a butcher chopping apart a carcass." We must give up, he said, "our 3,000-year-old habit of dichotomizing, splitting and separating in the style of Aristotelian logic. . . . Difficult though it may be, we must learn to think holistically rather than atomistically." In the same sense, in the context of Zen, Suzuki stated that the central fact of life "cannot be brought to the dissecting table of the intellect," and he said further: "To stop the flow of life and to look into it is not the business of Zen." Taking a metaphor from chess, Dr. Sidney Cohen described LSD perception as a kind of knight's-move thinking which leaps over logical premises and formal syllogisms. Huxley called for a recognition of the non-verbal humanities, or "the arts of being directly aware of the given facts of our existence." There is New Theology's emphasis upon "presentness" and here-now, derived especially from Bonhoeffer, Bultmann, and Buber. We could give many more examples, but perhaps we have made our point—that the psychic pendulum may be swinging again from the rational and the conscious to the intuitive and the unconscious, for better or for worse, resulting in a phenomenon which Maslow has termed "the current call back to raw experience as prior to any concepts or abstractions."

Our acceptance of the intellect's perceptions has always been tempered, to some degree at least, with doubt and uncertainty. Consider a nightmare. What does it represent, if not a temporary suspension of the natural order we normally perceive? And what does it express, if not a concealed fear that cause and effect are not wholly to be trusted or depended upon—that they may break down at any moment in waking life, leaving us naked and defenseless? We sense perhaps that the ordered universe with its immutable laws is not real at all but our own invention, and there is no guarantee that those laws tomorrow may not be rescinded. In the nightmare they are rescinded, revealing to us our subliminal anxiety.

But anxiety can turn to joy—and does so in the mystical, peak, and psychedelic experiences. We are suggesting, then, that there is a common factor in all of these meta-experiences. The common factor is an apparent suspension of cause and effect—and this in turn is the result of a temporary paralysis of the intellect, as Bergson defined the intellect. Simply that and nothing more—or that and nothing less. We are suggesting also, as indicated earlier, that the intellect is the basis for the myth of the Demiurge, that imperfect deity who is the cause of the fall from pure Being, the creation of matter, our phenomenal existence, and the Net of Illusion. And such an interpretation might well enable us to accommodate within the radical Western framework many fundamental doctrines of Eastern metaphysics. After all, it is possible to demythologize the East as well as the West, and such an effort now could lead at last to that reconciliation which has long been predicted.

In the East, as also in Plato's philosophy, the Net of Illusion has commonly been blamed on the body, or more specifically the senses, with the assertion that the world perceived by the senses is not real. The Eastern viewpoint has therefore appeared to be world-denying, and as such it has found small favor in the West, where men for the most part have obeyed an impulse to affirm the world, sorry as it may seem. But there is an alternative theory, and the contemporary meta-experience might seem to confirm it. It is not the body which is at fault, but only a *part* of the body: namely, the noetic brain, or that prefrontal bulge, pronounced in man, which accounts for the rational process and the rational way of viewing the world.

Thus the world itself is real enough; it is only our way of looking at the world which is not real. It is our mode of perception that leads us astray, and it is not the senses which deceive us but rather the mind or intellect which receives and interprets the sensory input. That evolutionary gift, the cerebral cortex, has enabled us so far to survive and to prosper, but it also has distorted our vision of ultimate reality. It directs our vision in such a way that we can see the world now only in a symbolic fashion, in terms of use and action. We know what happens, for example, when a man puts on a pair of those inverting spectacles which cause all images to appear upside down; after a time the man will adjust to the situation, and the images will appear to him right side up again. In the same way, perhaps, there is something which determines that we shall always see things in a certain manner: a kind of internal processing center for the raw data from the senses. No doubt this is for our own good, just as the rigid rules and the white lies of the parent are no doubt intended for the welfare of the child. But it is nevertheless restrictive, and it is based in a sense on a form of deceit.

It might be argued, then, that Eastern wisdom conceals an esoteric teaching along the lines of this same proposition. The East, it may be, has also meant *"as if."* The Net of Illusion does not refer to the world at all; it refers to our perception of the world. By the same token, OM is not an immaterial abstraction which transcends the world of matter and earthly existence; it is the world we live in but do not see: it is here-now, I-Thou, and "the reality that flows." Nirvana therefore does not imply a release from the body which leaves the world behind; it implies a mental or spiritual awakening which allows us to look at the world as it actually is. It does not deny the world. It affirms the world but rejects all partial views of it. It rejects the intellect, and it rejects the supposed order which intellect imagines it perceives in cause-and-effect relationships. As Spinoza suggested, this order perhaps is self-realizing. It is what we look for, what we are used to, and what we expect. If the world tomorrow should fall into disorder, we should soon perceive this too as perfect order.

In Mahayana Buddhism, the East itself has appeared to move toward a similar interpretation—from a denial of the world to a more perfect affirmation of the world—and this movement, as we have seen, comes to full expression in the teachings of Japanese Zen Buddhism. The goal of Zen is *satori.* And *satori* is not a denial of the world, nor is it a form of release from the world. It is, said Suzuki, *the acquiring of a new viewpoint.* It is a new way of looking at things, and it is designed specifically to overcome the intellect's way of looking at things. It is designed to destroy the intellect. As Suzuki put it: *"Satori* may be defined as intuitive looking-into, in contradiction to intellectual and logical understanding." It is not interested in concepts, abstractions, and a limited perception; "it does not

care so much for the elaboration of particulars as for a compre-
hensive grasp of the whole, and this intuitively." It is interested
in the here and now, and it accepts the world. "What was up
in the heavens, Zen has brought down to earth." It too proclaims
the reality that flows. Thus the Zen master denies that reality
is this, that, or the other thing; and when he is asked what
is left, he slaps his pupil and declares, "You fool, what is this?"
Satori, then, is a new kind of perception; but it is nevertheless
a perception of this world. "It is not that something different
is seen, but that one sees differently."

All this would seem to indicate that the radical West and
the demythologized East are not so far apart concerning the
Net of Illusion, and the worldly Westerner need not hesitate
for this reason to join that so-called leap to the East. From
Dietrich Bonhoeffer to James Bond, the contemporary emphasis
upon this world and this time is wholly compatible with the
esoteric interpretation of Eastern thought. In so far as they
confirm the reality of this world, the new insights into the
nature of meta-experiences challenge the orthodox Hindu as
much as they do the orthodox Baptist, and we may be experiencing today not so much a leap to the East as the emergence
at last of a possible East-West synthesis: a historic blending,
as it were, of the waters of the Jordan and the Ganges.

If the East and West should agree that the world is real,
however, where would this leave the question of immortality?
And what of reincarnation?

Reincarnation has been represented as a cycle of death and
rebirth, while nirvana has been represented as a release from
this cycle—and a release thereby from the world. After a final
death, according to the popular Western view, one merges with
the Absolute and thus achieves immortality in a state of pure

Being somewhere beyond the pitiful world of appearances and phenomena. We have said, however, that the world beyond the world of appearances is *this* world seen in a different way. We have said that nirvana is realized in this world by living men, not in some other world by dead men. *Nirvana is the pure experience of the present moment in this world here and now.* That at least was the esoteric interpretation, and we might very well ask, then, what this interpretation has to say on the question of death and immortality. Does it not in fact neglect the question altogether, leaving unanswered the fate of man when life is ended and death occurs?

The esoteric reply might be that life never ends and that death is just one more delusion of the intellect. Immortal life is not experienced in some ethereal realm beyond this world; it is experienced in this world, here, and that was the deeper meaning of the statement that nirvana is realized in this world by living men. To see the world as it really is means to understand that life is immortal. And thus the myth of the terrible wheel of death and rebirth. The wheel is caused by the intellect, and it is nothing more than the rational way of looking at things. The wheel is the I-It mind. It does not mean that we are cursed to return again and again to this world, for there is no other place we could possibly go. *There is only this world. There is nothing else.* The myth means that we are compelled by the intellect to go on and on imagining there is something else, and also to go on and on imagining the world exists as the intellect portrays it. To escape from the wheel means simply to become aware that the world it portrays is not the real world at all, or not the whole world. To escape from the wheel means to understand that death is false and that life is immortal. You shall know the truth and the truth shall set you free, from death as well as mechanism. If the intellect by nature cannot understand life, it follows that the intellect by nature cannot understand death. Its view of death results from the fact that it looks only at the parts, not at the Whole. If it would once look at the Whole, it would see immediately that life is immortal.

This interpretation would seem to justify immortality on a strictly monistic basis, by sacrificing pluralism; it preserves the One only by denying the reality of the individual selves. And what of the Western emphasis on personal survival of the individual self or soul? The esoteric doctrine would be that it is precisely our insistence on personal immortality which makes us blind to our actual immortality. The individual ego or personality has no real significance, and therefore the death of this personality has no real significance and should not be regretted. It is only because we insist on the significance of the one that the fact of the other seems so terribly important to us. And anyway, what do we really mean by personal? The truth is, the Western emphasis on this element has lately become at least somewhat less emphatic. In rejecting what he called the religious interpretation of Christianity, Bonhoeffer wrote from his prison in Berlin:

> In my view, that means to speak on the one hand metaphysically and on the other hand individualistically. Neither of these is relevant to the Bible message or to the man of today. Is it not true to say that individualistic concern for personal salvation has almost completely left us all? Are we not really under the impression that there are more important things than bothering about such a matter? (Perhaps not more important than the matter itself, but more than bothering about it.) I know it sounds pretty

monstrous to say that. But is it not, at bottom, even bibli-cal? Is there any concern in the Old Testament about saving one's soul at all? Is not righteousness and the King-dom of God on earth the focus of everything, and is not Romans 3.14 ff., too, the culmination of the view that in God alone is righteousness, and not in an individualistic doctrine of salvation? It is not with the next world that we are concerned, but with this world . . .

Tillich wrote:

> Even if the so-called arguments for the "immortality of the soul" had argumentative power (which they do not have) they would not convince existentially. For existenti-ally everybody is aware of the complete loss of self which biological extinction implies. The unsophisticated mind knows instinctively what sophisticated ontology formu-lates: that reality has the basic structure of self-world correlation and that with the disappearance of the one side, the world, the other side, the self, also disappears, and what remains is their common ground but not their structural correlation.

Again, what do we mean by personal—and by personal sur-vival? The meta-experience suggests that we are all expres-sions or aspects of a primary state of Being. And this is immor-tal. Therefore, we too are immortal—for we are it. In each of us the primary state comes briefly to a sharp focus: we sud-denly appear, like the dew that condenses from the still morn-ing air, or a wave that lifts from the surface of the sea. The dew burns away, the wave drops, and we die. But there is no real death. There is something elemental which survives and re-expresses itself. Thus a great actor might look back on the roles he has created and might also forget some of his lesser performances; but he does not imagine that he himself died with the closing of a play: he goes on, growing in talent, and even his failures may serve to instruct him. Similarly, what dies when a man dies is simply a role. What dies is merely a point of focus where Being had concentrated itself. What dies, in the last analysis, are only the particular memories which Being had accumulated at this point or that point, in this role or the other. And even the better of these are preserved by speech and by pen. What dies are only particular points of view. And the better of these are also preserved, for so long as they seem valid: until still better replace them.

All this is what the meta-experience seems to tell us, and no doubt it does not look very convincing or comforting on the printed page. Perhaps it appears to say only that life goes on— meaning that life goes on but you do not. But descriptions of the meta-experience are not the same as the experience, and the experience would seem to mean something more than life goes on: it would seem to mean that you go on too—although not in the traditional sense of reappearing somewhere after death with all of your thoughts, memories, and personal cachets intact. However desirable this latter kind of survival might normally appear to us, the fact remains that the meta-experiencer finds it neither desirable nor in any sense important. In a state of unsanity, it just doesn't matter.

Possibly the West could assimilate this interpretation of immortality, if it had to, since nobody really believes in personal survival anyway. We might be able to accept a monistic structure after death. What is far more difficult to accept is the thought that life has this character here upon the earth. The idea that other people do not really exist as separate entities can be a terrifying idea—pure hell, in fact—for it leaves you more alone even than Sartre would leave you. Not *we* are alone, with no excuses, but *I* am alone. There is an appalling difference between those two statements, and it is really the fundamental difference between the Western view and the Eastern. If life after death can be purchased only by paying the price of earthly pluralism, there are many perhaps who would not care to pay that price—who would give up the former, if they could, to retain the latter. And obviously you cannot have both a monistic immortality and a pluralistic mortality, since monistic survival is predicated on the assumption that life itself is monistic. There may therefore be a deep and basic wisdom reflected in the West's instinctive rejection of this horror. On the other hand, however, it could be a matter not of wisdom but of courage, or the lack of it: to say that the idea is terrifying is not to say that it is not true. In any case, it is a question to be faced—posed again now by the meta-experience. And it is hard. Very hard. This is why we said earlier that the Eastern challenge to pluralism is more critical even than the challenge to transcendence.

Meta-experience does not really deny the possibility of some unseen dimension which transcends the experience; it simply fails to provide us with any evidence to support the possibility —and, further, it does not suggest any *need* for this hypothesis. If there is a transcendent power, well and good. If not, that is all right too. The reality suggested by the experience is reality enough, if that is all there is, and the experience therefore has nothing to do with the existence or non-existence of a separate God. The experience tells us only that our normal perception of the world is limited and limiting: that we are deceived in our perception by a mental process, the seat of which can be anatomically localized in the human brain—which can even in fact be excised by surgery. The experience tells us to stop living only in the past and the future, or in a present moment which is perceived always in terms of the past and the future. It tells us that we need no longer be estranged from reality and from ourselves. The Eden story can now come to its inevitable and happy conclusion; the flaming sword has been extinguished, and we are free at last to re-enter the garden. It tells us this, and it does not tell us there is no transcendent God. After all, how could it? Negatives are hard to prove in any instance, and I cannot, for example, conclusively demonstrate that there is not at this moment a pink owl perched in a lime tree on the fifth moon of Jupiter. Nor do I especially care whether there is or isn't. But only a fool would insist that his vision necessarily takes in the whole of reality, and one wonders if God himself could ever be sure there was not somewhere some other God who transcends him. Thus the meta-experience tells us only what it sees; it speaks to us of this world—and it may be that this esoteric interpretation at least partially answers the objection of Tillich and Buber that mysticism is world-denying and therefore an inadequate response to existential anxiety.

The meta-experience, then, is not directly concerned with the question of God; but it is not for this reason any the less fundamental in its assertions. As William James put it to us, quoting Leuba: "Does God really exist? How does he exist? What is he? are so many irrelevant questions. Not God, but life, more life, a larger, richer, more satisfying life, is, in the last analysis, the end of religion. The love of life, at any and every level of development, is the religious impulse."

Let us assume, for the sake of argument, that the meta-experience offers an accurate perception of ultimate reality. We still must ask whether it is wise or prudent to seek that experience and achieve that perception.

For one thing, the experience suggests that symbols serve only to distort our view of the actual world. But I can never forget Helen Keller's story of that day at the well house, at the age of seven, when she first learned the meaning of language. Before that, she said, she had been only a wild little animal lost in the dark, unable to give love or receive it. "Before that supreme event there was nothing in me except the instinct to eat and drink and sleep. My days were a blank, without past, present, or future, without hope or anticipation, without interest or joy." Then Anne Sullivan held one of her hands under the running pump, and into the other she spelled out "w-a-t-e-r." The meta-experiencer would say of course that "w-a-t-e-r" and water are two different things; but Miss Keller has given us her own reaction. "I knew then that 'w-a-t-e-r' meant the wonderful cool something that was flowing over my hand. That living word awakened my soul, gave it light, hope, joy, set it free!" Or again: "All at once there was a strange stir within me —a misty consciousness, a sense of something remembered. . . . Nothingness was blotted out. . . . That word 'water' dropped into my mind like the sun in a frozen winter world." And we might do well to remember this before we decide to blow out that sun.

An obvious objection to the meta-experience is that it denies or ignores the existence of evil—which it considers simply a dualistic deception. And this was the main objection James had to the optimistic mysticism of Whitman. You cannot ignore evil, said James, for "the skull will grin in at the banquet." "Here on our very hearths and in our gardens," he said, "the infernal cat plays with the panting mouse, or holds the hot bird fluttering in her jaws. Crocodiles and rattlesnakes and pythons are at this moment vessels of life as real as we are; their loathsome existence fills every minute of every day that drags its length along." For his part, James preferred an optimism which first acknowledged evil and yet saw hope. Only this could we really trust.

There are the clear and present dangers which threaten the individual who is in the grips of a meta-experience: running in front of cars, leaping from windows with the expectation of flying, a generalized indifference to injury and death. But there is also a less clear and even more present danger which threatens the vitality and welfare of society itself, and this is the danger of a quietistic indifference to social goals and social rewards. Until very recently there was little cause for concern about this, and Maslow provides us with an excellent example. While he conceded there was a possible quietistic danger inherent in the peak experience, he added that the experience came rarely even to self-actualizing people, and as late as 1962 he wrote: "Therefore the problem posed here is more an ultimate than an immediate one, more a theoretical problem than a practical one." Now LSD has made the problem both immediate and practical, and the issue must be dealt with.

Prohibitive laws are one answer, and certainly there is little to be said for the so-called Gumball Machine theory that psychedelics should be freely dispensed to the general population, with no restrictions. We do after all have gun laws (though not very good ones); we have laws regarding the purchase and consumption of liquor; and there are regulations and licensing procedures for people who want to drive autos or fly airplanes. In view of the potential dangers of an immediate nature, it might seem fair to put psychedelics in the same category as alcohol, guns, planes, and cars. But in fact the governmental response has been to outlaw them almost altogether. This apparently has succeeded only in frustrating some very important research by scientists, and it is doubtful in any case whether legal measures can resolve the more basic questions that are raised by the drug movement.

There is the other side of the Delphic coin. *Know Thyself,* yes. But also *Nothing in Excess.* As Suzuki put it: "There is also such a thing as too much attachment to the experience of *satori,* which is to be detested." This appears to be a very neat answer, but it is much too easy telling people to behave themselves, and urging moderation in this thing of all things is no solution. LSD may not be addictive, but truth is.

This brings us to the test James suggested for the revelations of drunkenness. "If merely 'feeling good' could decide," said James, "drunkenness would be the supremely valid human experience." The question is—does the experience work out when it is inserted into the environment? This is another way of asking whether the individual continues to function and survive, and whether or not the world's work still gets done.

But the psychedelic quietist would reply that none of these things matters. It is the environment that is out of joint, and the world's work is ridiculous. As for survival, life is eternal—especially so for a psychic mutant. And just by the way, there is nothing evil about pythons and rattlesnakes.

This is not to say that all drug cultists are quietists. In fact, there is a fundamental dichotomy within the drug movement, and this is reflected in the programs and philosophies of the two major psychedelic churches—the Church of the Awakening and the Neo-American Church—that existed before Timothy

Leary's League for Spiritual Discovery was founded in 1966. The Church of the Awakening, mentioned earlier, might be described as the middle-class right wing of the movement. Many of its members are businessmen or professional people, and the church insists that even psychedelic religion has both an internal and an external function—the latter to be expressed in terms of "love," "service," and "growth." In its statement of purpose, the church adds:

> It is important to recognize and to understand the existence of these two functions, internal and external; to recognize that we have a basic need and urge to *learn,* and an equally basic one to *serve,* to share. Next, of course, there must be an aspiration of the achievement of these objectives within the heart of each of us. And then, this knowledge and aspiration must be channeled into action. We must *do* something about it!

The Neo-American Church, on the other hand, represents more or less the bohemian left wing of the drug movement. It would seem to be dedicated only to "the appreciation of Transcendental Reality," and, although the church officially advocates a kind of revolutionary nihilism, the membership in general appears to be more interested in withdrawal than revolt. The inclination is to "turn on and drop out." There are individual exceptions, of course, but this is the overall impression one gets.

The Neo-American Church to date has received far more publicity than the Church of the Awakening has, and it has been more aggressive in recruiting new members—particularly among the young. While a cleavage does exist, then, it would seem nevertheless that there are now many more quietists than activists within the drug movement as a whole, and the problem grows more pressing with every day that passes.

The psychedelic quietist of course does not consider his attitude a problem—he considers it a solution—and in fact he might argue that there is precedent for his decision to withdraw from the mainstream, renouncing the goals and rewards of society. Would not identical consequences follow if Christians started to take the New Testament literally?

The quietist asserts that there is no destination ahead of us; we are already there. He announces, in effect, that he is getting off the bus.

It may be, then, that the question comes down to this: Is the cosmic bus going anywhere?

13 OM or Omega?

There may often be good reasons for bad laws. The sexual act, for example, is condoned only if the partners involved are a male and a female who are married (to each other), and any deviation from that pattern is proscribed as sinful and evil. It is difficult to believe, however, that there is anything intrinsically wicked in the performance of a mechanical act engaged in by consenting partners. Young people especially are more and more inclined to ask, "Why not?" And the reasons offered are not very convincing.

But the reasons offered may not be the real reasons.

Human society is founded pragmatically on the family unit, and it has therefore been necessary to encourage matrimony and to challenge at once any conduct or philosophy which appears to threaten the stability of that institution. Thus the marriage

216

relationship is represented as the only legitimate source of sexual gratification, and thus also the myth is promulgated that sex outside the marriage bed is a personal sin against your body and soul—a violation of heavenly law. But the law is man-made, not celestial, and the sin in fact may be real enough—but it is social, not personal. It is a sin against the social structure and therefore a sin against the common good. Such an idea of course is hard to convey, and society (or life) has relied instead upon a necessary fiction. There are many today who recognize the fiction and who seek to destroy it; but they fail to recognize the reason for the fiction, or the purpose it has served, or the problems involved in replacing it. Their efforts therefore are met with a blind and instinctive resistance, which they assess as mere prudishness. But it is more than prudishness; it is life trying to protect itself, as best it can, in the only way it knows how.

In the same sense, perhaps, there would appear to be an instinctive reaction against the drug movement's monistic pronouncements—as also its quietistic emphasis upon the pure experience of the here-now present moment. Assuming that life (or society) has some dumb understanding of its own welfare, or its own destiny, we might inquire into the source of this reaction.

As for monism, an analogy could be made to the human body and the cells which compose it. The body is a monistic whole in which the cells all partake, although the cells can have no notion of that fact: each is assigned its specialized function, thus enabling the body to go about its business. What would happen, then, if these dutiful cells or selves should somehow gain awareness of the greater Self in which they participate? What would happen if they ceased their functioning to contemplate the body? Most likely, the body would not like that very much and would order the cells to stop it at once. For the greater Self has its greater business to attend to. If the hand indeed is divided into five fingers, the better to do its work, this clearly implies, does it not, that there is work to be done? And it cannot be done if the fingers are curled inward in a self-admiring fist.

A similar interpretation is possible in the case of "presentness." As we have seen, a here-now rejection of the intellect's perception is a rejection in essence of the past and the future—especially the future—and this brings us again to another East-West dichotomy which seems at least to be basic in nature. It is said that the orthodox East looks backward to a primordial totality (and in this sense perhaps it acknowledges the past, but not in the sense of using the past to predict future action). The demythologized East does not look backward; but neither does it look forward: it is concerned alone with the here-now present moment. This is another way of saying that it accepts the status quo. The West on the other hand looks both backward and forward—but especially forward. It looks to the future. And it does so with the implication that there is unfinished business to be conducted there; otherwise its constant peering into the future is a matter simply of perceptual deception, as charged.

Thus the myth of the Demiurge comes into conflict with the myth of Ulysses.

The Ulysses myth is a Western myth. It does not accept the status quo of the present moment but suggests instead that life is evolving. This process in turn points toward a future purpose, and acceptance of the present moment would defeat that purpose. Darwin of course showed that life is constantly transforming itself—changing its forms, in the manner of Proteus—but he failed to show that it is truly evolving in the sense of having a definite direction, purpose, and goal. Others in the West, however, have said that life is evolving in precisely this sense. Hegel has said it, Nietzsche has said it, Bergson has said it, Altizer has said it, Maslow has said it—and Teilhard de Chardin has said it.

Hegel depicted the universe as an absolute Mind which is seeking to fulfill itself and know itself. Nietzsche proclaimed the Overman and the will to power; man is but a bridge, he said, and life is that which must ever surpass itself. Bergson spoke of a vital force which advances, creatively, toward a distant future end which cannot be predicted because it is not predetermined. Altizer asserted that God himself is evolving, from transcendence to immanence, and he specifically rejected "the backward movement of Oriental mysticism." He rejected the orthodox Eastern view of a "lost paradise" we can only regain through "a reversal of the cosmos." "Above all," said Altizer, "a reborn and radical Christian faith must renounce every temptation to return to an original or primordial sacred, or to follow a backward path leading to an earlier and presumably purer form of the Word." In the same context, Maslow has distinguished between Being and Becoming; between a "high Nirvana" and "low Nirvana"; between the "the Heaven ahead" (of growth) and "the Heaven behind" (of regression). Nowhere in recent times, however, has the concept of a goal-directed cosmos been given richer expression than is found in the metaphysical system of the scientist-priest Teilhard, who developed a profoundly unorthodox theory of universal evolution.

Teilhard, a Jesuit, had been forbidden to publish that theory during his lifetime; but his views have attracted widespread attention since his death in 1955, and respect for his system has continued to grow both inside and outside the Roman Catholic Church. For many of the faithful, with the passage of time, Teilhard's ideas have appeared to be more and more profound and less and less unorthodox—which is hardly surprising, for they represent in fact an attempted reconciliation of scientific knowledge and religious tradition. It is difficult to say whether Teilhard was a mystical scientist or a scientific mystic, but he is worth listening to in either case. He speaks to the contemporary situation. And what is more, he addresses himself directly to the issues raised by psychedelic quietism.

Teilhard proposed, to start, that evolution is not just willy-nilly Darwinian transformism. It has a definite direction.

In the beginning, in the primordial chaos, the individual particles of unorganized matter contained certain elementary "liberties," but matter by and large was subject to the laws of chance and statistical determinism. After a time, however, the particles began to organize—first in simple forms, then in complex forms. As eons passed, the forms became increasingly complex. And this complexity resulted at last in a new phenomenon: it resulted in consciousness. For consciousness is a product of complexity.

At first there was a primitive animal consciousness. Then, further complexification produced the human brain—and rational consciousness. For the first time, evolution became aware of itself.

This, then, is evolution's direction: toward increasing complexity and (as a result) increasing consciousness. Thus, by tracing the pattern of *psychical* rather than *physical* development, Teilhard laid the basis for a neo-anthropocentricity which restores man to the center of things as the most complex and conscious creation. Man is not just a speck lost in a remote corner of infinite space. If the universe is a super-organism which is in the process now of realizing itself, then man is the "head" of that organism.

But evolution did not stop with the emergence of the human brain. From that point on, complexification continued in the form of *social organization* and human technology. Teilhard saw no reason to distinguish these from "natural" (biological) evolution; for there is nothing unnatural in nature, and the wireless is simply an extension of the evolving human mind. The computer and the space probe are similar extensions, Teilhard would have insisted, had he lived to see their era, for what do they represent if not an enlargement of our total awareness? By the same logic, government at all levels is an expansion of overall consciousness, through complexification, which allows us to deal with an ever wider area of concern, and the United Nations may be the harbinger of a global mind with global awareness.

As we saw in an earlier chapter, Teilhard held that this process is directed from within by an indwelling Christ who took charge of evolution by partially inserting himself into matter. Teilhard stated further that the process will lead eventually to a final state of super-organization and super-awareness he referred to as the Omega point. At this stage, in a hyper-centration of cosmic matter, mankind will reflect upon itself at a single point—and will leave the earth behind to become pure spirit. Mankind will abandon this world to rejoin the godhead—not by space ship, but spiritually and inwardly.

Ideally, this should happen. But, said Teilhard, there is no predestined guarantee that this will happen. The Omega point must be attained by conscious effort. And already there are ominous portents. Even now, "a whirlpool is beginning to appear ahead of us, in the stream that carries us along."

In a magnificent construction, Teilhard divided the human race into two camps, the pessimists and the optimists, and the latter camp he divided into buddhists, pluralists, and monists.

Man must choose his evolutionary path, said Teilhard. And each of these divisions represents a potential choice or possible path.

1. The first choice is pessimism or optimism. The question in this case is fundamental, and it is simply Hamlet's question asked on a grand scale. To Be or not to Be? That is the question the whole universe must ask itself. Does it make any sense to exist, or would it be better perhaps if there was no life at all? In the early stages of evolution, the universe instinctively chooses life over non-life and Being over non-Being; it instinctively chooses to Be. But what happens when life becomes conscious and therefore aware of itself? Is it not possible that Being will reject its own existence, seeing no point to it all, and that thinking men will go on strike against an evolutionary course which seems to have no real meaning and no final purpose? Even now the world has split into two opposing factions, and those in one faction say that life is not worthwhile. Why bother, then, to go any further? These are the pessimists; let us leave them behind.

2. That leaves the optimists, and they must choose between the optimism of withdrawal and the optimism of evolution. The optimists of withdrawal are the buddhists, who wish to quit the world at once; they acknowledge that Being as Being is good, but they deny that the awareness of true Being can be found in the forward-looking world of appearances. There is nowhere to go, they say. We are already there. The idea of a goal ahead is

222

delusional, they say, and we need only to realize this; the solution, it follows, is to "break away from the evolutionary determinism, break the spell, withdraw." Let them cut the threads, then, and let them retire to their future-denying nirvana.

3. That leaves the optimists of evolution: "the believers in some ultimate value in the tangible evolution of things." They are faithful to the future, "faithful to Earth." But they too have a decision to make, and their choice is between pluralism and monism. The pluralists are concerned primarily with their personal freedom and individual uniqueness, "in opposition to others." For the monists, "nothing exists or finally matters except the Whole." Which shall it be? "This," said Teilhard, "is the ultimate choice, by way of which Mankind must finally be divided, knowing its own mind." And Teilhard, for his part, chose monism.

Only in union, said Teilhard, can man ever hope to achieve his final destiny, and a separatist individualism is ultimately self-destructive: "the element burns up all its future in a flying spark." Let us plunge forward into monism, "even though something in us perish." For it is written that he who loses his soul shall save it—and in true associations, as opposed to collective heaps, the combination of separate elements does not eliminate their differences. It exalts them. As in the specialized cells of the body, "true union differentiates." This is true even in the case of the anthill or beehive—the palace of honey— where specialization is based upon such biological functions as nutrition and reproduction. How much truer it must be, then, in the case of a *spiritual* association in which individual personalities will conspire together to create "a common consciousness." In such a union "each element achieves completeness, not directly in a separate consummation, but by incorporation in a higher pole of consciousness in which alone it can enter into contact with all others." Tillich was expressing the same thought when he denied that union with the Ground of Being means a loss of self in a larger whole. "If the self participates in the power of being-itself," said Tillich, "it receives itself back. For the power of being acts through the power of the individual selves. It does not swallow them as every limited whole, every collectivism, and every conformism does."

Teilhard died before psychedelic quietism became an issue, but his second set of alternatives—withdrawal or evolution—goes nevertheless to the heart of that issue. And Teilhard has not left us to wonder which of the two alternatives he would recommend as the proper and logical choice. This is implicit, he said, in the fact that life up to now has followed "a precise line of direction." There has been an unmistakable progression toward an increase of consciousness and a greater awareness. What we must do, therefore, is select that path which points ahead in the same direction—"the one which seems best able to develop and preserve in us the highest degree of consciousness."

It might be argued that the meta-experience represents an advanced level of consciousness, as opposed to a regression, and it is possible even to interpret Eastern doctrine as evolutionary. There is, for example, the concept of "the days and nights of Brahma," contained in the Hindu holy book, the *Bhagavad-Gita*. This suggests the image mentioned earlier of a games-playing God who acts out the cosmic drama for his own amusement, pretending to be Many when actually he is One. The drama continues for a thousand ages—until the Self-deception is at last revealed, and the One once more is aware of his Oneness. Whereupon the whole cycle is repeated, forever and ever. There is some support for this idea in the modern astrophysical theory of an "oscillating" universe, which holds that all of the galaxies comprising the universe were once contained in a primordial atom of incredible density. At some point in the past this atom exploded, sending all the raw material of the universe flying out into space—the galaxies evolving with the passage of time. There is considerable evidence that this so-called expansion of the universe is still going on—in fact there seems little doubt of it—but recent observations indicate that the outward flight of the galaxies will one day slow to a stop, and the universe will then contract again into a new primordial atom. Indeed, the process may have occurred countless times already since the dawn of creation. Or so we are told. The theory is based, I believe, on the estimated force of the original impetus and the estimated amount of stellar material.

No doubt science has weighed and measured the universe very accurately and thus can predict what it will do some billions of years from now. But it might be easier to accept the idea of oscillation as final if science were just a trifle more accurate in predicting tomorrow's weather in Omaha. Will it rain there or won't it? However that may be, we have already seen the danger of marrying physics to metaphysics (in connection with free will), and it is doubtful in any case that Eastern evolution is anything like Western evolution. The Eastern future is not a creative future, in the Western sense, but rather an eternal repetition of the past. This does not mean the East is wrong and the West is right, but it does mean there is an essential difference in their assertions on this point. The Western future is clearly denied both by Eastern metaphysics and by psychedelic quietism.

Shall we rest on our oars? Are we already there?

Addressing himself to the buddhists among us, Teilhard

agreed that the concept of an ultimate withdrawal from the phenomenal rat race "fits in very well with the *final* demands of a world of evolutionary structure." But he made one proviso: "that the world in question shall have reached a stage of development so advanced that its 'soul' can be detached without losing any of its completeness, as something wholly formed." And to this he added:

> But have we any reason to suppose that human consciousness *today* has achieved so high a degree of richness and perfection that it can derive nothing more from the sap of the earth? Again we may turn to history for an answer. Let us suppose, for example, that the strivings and the progress of civilization had come to an end at the time of Buddha, or in the first centuries of the Christian era. Can we believe that nothing essential, of vision and action and love, would have been lost to the Spirit of Earth? Clearly we cannot. And this simple observation alone suffices to guide our decision. So long as a fruit continues to grow and ripen we refrain from picking it. In the same way, so long as the world around us continues, even in suffering and disorder, to yield a harvest of problems, ideas and new forces, it is a sign that we must continue to press forward in the conquest of matter. Any immediate withdrawal . . . would certainly be premature.

He also said, elsewhere: "God creates and shapes us through the process of evolution. . . . God awaits us when the evolutionary process is complete; to rise above the world, therefore, does not mean to despise or reject it, but to pass through it and sublime it."

Teilhard may or may not have demonstrated that evolution

has a goal or a purpose. It is possible, however, that he did show evolution to have at least a direction, and that alone would be no small gift in this age of uncertainty. Given a sense of direction, if nothing else, there are many perhaps who would be willing, in an act of faith, to accept the idea of an unguessed future purpose. And after all, at this stage in our development, who has the wisdom to deny that possibility? Is anyone so all-knowing, when all of us together would seem to know so little?

If we are estranged from one level of reality and locked in a world of action, it may be that we are estranged for a reason— and a reason, moreover, which we cannot yet foresee. If there is a Whole which is seeking to know itself, it may be that the Whole aspires to a more perfect knowledge of its parts as well as its Oneness—that the Whole demands of us that we first conquer the earth, moon, and stars before we turn inward. If there is a deeper level of reality, revealed by psychedelics, there could well be another level still deeper than that. Anything and everything is possible, and nothing as yet is impossible. This is not to say that the psychedelic insight is not true; we are merely suggesting that it may not be the whole truth. If a little learning is a dangerous thing, there is danger indeed in any total commitment to a partial understanding, and some of the drug cultists might at least be a little less cavalier in their decision to reverse the apparent direction of the universal tides. Perhaps some knowledge comes to us too soon, before we know how to use it or what to make of it, as was certainly true with the atom. But it is too late for regrets, in the case of the atom or the case now at hand. A decision of some sort must obviously be made, and it is essentially a very simple decision—though by no means an easy one.

Backward to OM? Or forward to Omega?

Shall we accept the myth of the Demiurge, which suggests that our salvation lies in the simple acceptance of the here-now present moment—concealed by the intellect? Or shall we accept the myth of Ulysses, which suggests that life is a process of evolutionary growth toward some distant future goal we cannot as yet perceive? These are the central questions posed at this time by the mystical, peak, and LSD experiences.

Teilhard felt that mankind as a whole has reached its decision and has chosen its path. If that choice in fact has been made, as he supposed, then it is much easier to understand society's angry and dogmatic reaction to those uncompromising individuals who insist that the meta-experience points toward a total withdrawal and nowhere else.

When Ulysses found his men feeding upon the flowery food, in the land of the lotus eaters, he did not pause for thought. He asked them no questions, and he offered them no arguments. He laid hold of the men, and he led them, weeping and sore against their will, back to the swift ships.

He knew where he was going. He was going to Ithaca.

Postscript

"Four o'clock, and all's wrong."

So says the voice on the tape recorder as I listen to it now. My voice.

Having been reminded often enough of those schoolmen who would not look through Galileo's telescope, I participated in a psychedelic experiment on May 16, 1966, at the Ridgeway psychiatric hospital in Chicago. Present were Dr. A. I. Jackman, a psychiatrist; Dr. Herbert Maltz, clinical director of the hospital, and a psychedelic guide I shall refer to here as Jim. We used Huxley's drug, mescaline, because LSD at that time had been taken off the legal market. The two produce identical effects, I was told, the only difference being that a much stronger dosage is required in the case of mescaline, which is administered in milligrams rather than micrograms. I was first given a thorough medical examination, including an electro-cardiogram, and we then retired to a small but pleasantly furnished consultation room on the second floor of the hospital, where the drapes were drawn against the afternoon sunlight. At 2 P.M. Dr. Jackman handed me a paper cup of water and five white capsules, each of them containing seventy milligrams of mescaline; a half-hour later I took two more capsules, for a total dose of 490 milligrams.

Nothing happened for more than an hour.

Before going further, I should speak very briefly about myself and various subjective factors which may have influenced my reaction to the drug. While I had always been interested in the implications of religious perception, I was not normally given to mystical states of mind; some slight significance might be attached here, however, to a phenomenon I had experienced occasionally since early childhood. This would happen once or twice a year, I suppose, and would last ten or fifteen seconds at most. In moments of abstraction, my immediate environment would suddenly appear to take on a new and wordless meaning I could not define; time would stop, all objects would lose their names, and the world would seem somehow peaceful and perfect. The landscape would first appear to blur, as if the film in a movie projector had jumped its track, and then it would come clear again in a slightly different focus: it would look quite the same as before, but in some subtle way its meaning would have changed. Just how is hard to say.

I had always had vivid memories of my infancy, including a few sunlit memories of the cradle itself in the very first days of my life, and the experience often reminded me of those pristine recollections—of that holy time, at the dawn of life, when I lay innocent in sunbeams. Curiously, certain pieces of music would often serve to evoke the experience: *Clair de lune,* for one, which I always associated with sunlight, and "Zing Went the Strings of My Heart." I never supposed that the experience was important, and I never mentioned it to anybody, although I did give it a name. I called it "the Shift." I had never heard of a peak experience, of course, and maybe it was something of the sort; maybe it was a pint-size *satori.* In any case, it occurred less frequently as I grew older. I became a newspaperman, and newspapermen are not very mystical. I was taught to be critical and objective, and I was prepared to be both when I swallowed the seven capsules.

The atmosphere of a psychiatric hospital was far from ideal for a psychedelic setting, but I knew at least that I was in good hands should anything go wrong, and I felt no apprehension whatever about taking the drug. In fact, I had been looking forward to it. I had read many accounts of good trips and bad trips, and I fully expected to experience an ego loss, but that prospect didn't trouble me. Finally, I should point out that I had recently been reading a fair amount of Eastern literature, and indeed I had just reread the *Tibetan Book of the Dead.*

After about seventy minutes, Jim told me, "You look different." I asked him in what way I looked different, and he said, "You're somehow younger." I smiled and pointed to a framed picture hanging on one wall. "That water stain on the left-hand side of the glass," I said. "Was that there before?"

"I think something is beginning to happen to you," said Dr. Jackman.

Twenty minutes later I felt a numbness creeping over my body, and I said that I seemed to be losing my muscular control. "But again, nothing special." I yawned and added: "That's interesting. The coffee in this cup looks green . . . sort of a greenish cast to it." I had been chain-smoking cigarettes, and I told Jim apologetically: "I don't want to put out the last cigarette. I'm such a smoker. I keep thinking just one more cigarette before . . ." Jim reached down and switched on a tape recorder, filling the room with symphonic music set at low volume. That annoyed me for some reason. It seemed prearranged. "Jim," I told him, "your whiskers have got a greenish tint to them."

I had been sitting on a long couch, my knees crossed, head nodding. I felt so weak and listless, as if I hadn't slept for days. "Jim," I said, "did you usually start with visual things? I've been waiting for colors." I looked down at my tweed jacket and my green-and-white striped shirt, then farther down at my crossed legs. Black pants, black socks, black shoes. The only trouble was, the legs weren't mine. They looked alien and somehow sinister. I knew they were attached to my body, and I knew I could move them, but they weren't my legs. They weren't *me*. Or better yet, I wasn't *them*. It was just as if I were looking at the legs of some stranger sitting next to me in a bar, or on a train. So primly crossed. So black. And the silk-hosed ankles, so damned self-satisfied. I didn't like them at all. "I didn't think my legs looked like that," I said. "I thought they looked different . . . but the point is, I'm about one quarter-inch outside myself now. That's how I feel, I mean. I'm sitting here, but I've also moved about a quarter-inch outside my body, and that's why I can look at my body now and see it just the same way other people see it. Funny, too. I'd expected all these visual things first. Colors . . . jewels."

So tired. So numb. Just one more cigarette.

Jim helped me off with my jacket and shoes, and I stretched out on the couch. I complained again about my lack of motor control, and Dr. Maltz had me tug at his fingers and then press my open palm against his palm in an effort to resist it. "You have not actually lost any strength," he said. Then he tested me with a pin, jabbing at the back of my hand with the dull end and sharp end. I told him each time which end it was, and finally I said, "That hurt—but so what?" I felt the pain, but it didn't matter.

Jim had turned up the music. The whole long-playing tape seemed to be Beethoven, and I didn't like it. The *Eroica* in particular sounded ponderous and threatening. Nothing human there; it was pure mathematics, written on Olympus. "Feel good," I said. "Feel different. It's like, ah . . ." I opened my eyes. "I feel like I got great big hands. You know? When I open my eyes, I'm back in the room. And everything looks normal. When I close them, though, I feel sort of disembodied. And I'm not sure yet which way I want to go. Maybe I'd rather stay here and watch it happen. I have the feeling I'd drift off if I closed my eyes. It's just a question of whether I want to get disembodied or not. I have the feeling that . . . I have the feeling that . . . It's very relaxing. Especially in the small of the back. It's like I'm floating in clouds without any body, and it's very nice to get rid of your body. I feel this loss of weight and loss of tension, like it all ran out of me. Especially in the small of the back. That's where I'd localize it. It's like I drank a hundred martinis without passing out. Still able to think and remember. It's like being drunk without being drunk. You know? But just the same, I don't feel all that great . . . feel different."

I rolled to one side and started to repeat the first-person pronoun, nominative case. "I, I, I . . . I, I, I . . . I, I, I . . . Ai, Ai, Ai . . . Yi, Yi, Yi . . . Ai-Yi-Yi-Yi . . . Yo, Yo, Yo . . . Yo, Yo, Yo . . . Spanish for I . . . Yo, Yo, Yo . . . Yo-Yo, Yo-Yo . . . capitalized trademark . . . Duncan Yo-Yo . . . That's it, we're all Duncan

Yo-Yos. Spanish word for I, means we're all a bunch of Yo-Yos. Up and down on a string. Conclusive proof of Leary's Game Theory. . . . But not really, of course."

Struck by a sudden thought, I sat up in alarm.

"What happened?'" I asked. "What happened to all the other people?"

I was still puzzling that over when my gaze fell again on the cold black dregs in my coffee cup. I stuck a finger in the coffee and became a continuum with it and the plastic cup. "Ah, it feels so good . . . so good. I feel real good. Dr. Jackman, you're a Yo-Yo." I knew I was being obnoxious, and I didn't like that, either. "When does everything start to get exquisite?" I asked. "Nothing I expected has happened yet. This is a bore, so far." I fell back helplessly on the couch, and Dr. Jackman told me, "You're just at the beginning."

"The beginning?"

I drifted off, mumbling incoherently, and the doctors left. I was alone now with Jim. "Poor little world," I said. "Poor little world . . . poor little world." Later I opened my eyes and found that Jim had gone, too. I sat up and looked around for him, rubbing my eyes with my fists. But the room was deserted.

"Jim? Did you go away, Jim, or are you really here? Maybe you're still here, and I just can't see you. Could it actually happen? Of course it couldn't. But then, how can I tell? I'm under the influence of a drug. Oh, you shouldn't have gone away, Jim. Did you go away, or didn't you? Are you there, Jim? Where are you?"

The door opened. Jim came in.

"I went to the washroom," he said. "Is something the matter?"

"No," I said. "Everything's fine."

A nurse brought us a meal, which we ate at the desk. Corned

beef hash, apricots, sliced pickles, and another pot of coffee. I shoveled the food down impersonally, much as you would stoke a furnace, and the process of eating seemed highly humorous. Biting into the pickles, I could sense their molecular structure; I had a mouth full of cells and atoms, I thought, and I could feel my teeth grinding them about. How ridiculous chewing was. It would have been much easier, I thought, simply to slip the pickles in through my ribs. I knew it wouldn't work if I tried it, but I thought nevertheless that it should work. After all, there was no such thing as a solid; there were only those spinning atoms, which in turn were only sparks of energy (whatever that was), and the emptiness of the atomic inner space must surely be calculated in millions and billions of micromiles. I stuck my finger in the coffee again—it was hot this time, but that didn't matter—and I imagined that the end of my finger had disappeared. I laughed and said that Huxley hadn't turned into a coffee cup, had he? I, on the other hand, had just turned into a coffee cup. Which is to say, I and the coffee cup were the same thing, really; where the one ended, the other began. The coffee cup, you might say, had turned into me. Certainly the pickles and hash had turned into me, and those Hindus clearly had known what they were talking about: it was all a case of food living on food, and after that becoming food.

After the meal I lay down again and shut my eyes. In the darkness of my mind I saw a Technicolor display of weird-looking growths waving about, like plants in a current at the bottom of the sea. There were stalks and sponges and fan-shaped objects: pink and green and purple. I thought I might wander around down there for several centuries, and I wasn't at all sure that I wanted to. I thought about my family, and it didn't seem fair to go away so long and leave them behind—like Rip Van

Winkle. What if they needed me for something, and what if they were all dead when I finally came back? "Those are organisms," I said, imagining now that I had recognized the growths. "I am looking inside my own eyeball. And those all are parts of my eyeball."

Then I lay still for a time, drifting, and Jim supposed that I was past the point of no return, comfortable and happy. Coming up quietly, he slipped a set of stereophonic earphones onto my head, the big foam-rubber phones snapping over my ears in a snug fit. A majestic Beethoven chord exploded inside my brain, and I instantly disappeared. My body no longer existed, and neither did the world. The world and I had been utterly annihilated. I could feel the pressure of the earphones; but in the space between the phones, where my head should have been, there was absolutely nothing . . . *nothing!* I was Mind alone, lost in an icy blue grotto of sound. There was only the music, and then bright colors that turned out to be musical notes. The notes danced along a silver staff of music that stretched from one eternity to another, beyond the planets and stars and space itself. Red notes. Blue notes. But they had no substance or dimension, and nothing was real in that empty cavern between the two earphones. That unbounded abyss. The music rolled on in orgiastic waves of sound and color, and then I myself was one of the notes. I was being swept along on the silver staff, at twice the speed of light, rushing farther and farther away from my home back there in the Milky Way. In desperation, at the last possible moment, I reached up with hands I did not own, and I tore off the earphones.

I was back in the room. But from that point on, it went wrong.

I sat in a chair, staring at the floor. Jim pulled back the

drapes, filling the room with the last light of day. Outside in the streets I could hear auto horns honking, and once a fire engine went by. I felt a terrible depression rising slowly from the bottom of my soul.

"Even out here where I am," I said, "I don't know what's going on."

Nobody knew what was going on. Nobody knew anything.

It seemed to me that my sense of self was completely gone now. It had been ripped away by the music, and I had come back without it. Although I knew nothing, I felt that some awful truth was about to be revealed to me. It was lurking somewhere just beyond the borders of my comprehension, and very soon now I should have to come face to face with it.

I studied the room, and I realized that I now formed a continuum with everything in sight. The room seemed to shimmer in the dying rays of sunlight, and I was aware once more of the atomic substructure that underlay the visible world of the senses. It struck me that the visible world was wholly real, and in no way a deception, but it nevertheless had this underlying structure which glowed and pulsed like a living force. And it all ran together in a single composition. This is hard to describe, and the only analogy I can think of is in painting—for example, Seurat's huge pointillist canvas, "A Sunday Afternoon on the Grande Jatte." The figures on the grass are real enough, and there is a logic to their placement and development; if you look closely, however, you will see that the figures and the grass and the sparkling water are all composed of tiny dots of color, and these dots all blend together to form a single scene and a single reality. The lady with her parasol looks out at the sailboats on the water, and she imagines perhaps that they are far away and separate; but everything on the canvas is inexorably locked to-

gether in one flowing creation, and the lady in fact is an extension of the parasol, water, and boats. I thought of that canvas
as I sat in the room, drugged out of my mind, and it seemed to
me that I was locked into my scene just as inexorably as Seurat's
figures were locked into theirs. Dots of energy or dots of paint,
it was all the same. But even this seemed unsatisfactory, the
more I thought of it, and then I remembered those Van Gogh
canvases in which sky and earth swirl together like magnetic
force fields. "That's it," I thought. "The reality that flows . . .
much better than dots." And I pitied poor Van Gogh, if that was
his constant perception. Those raging cypress trees, like tongues
of green flame licking at the heavens—those whirling suns. No
wonder he cut off his ear.

I tried to explain it to Jim.

"Instead of trying to figure it out," he said, "just try to feel
what's happening."

But I didn't like what was happening. I was starting to remember something, and it seemed to have some connection with
sunlight and a cradle. But what could it be? Then it came to
me that I was gradually remembering my own identity, like an
amnesia victim who slowly recovers his past. Finally it all fell
together, and I remembered who I was. And it was so simple,
really. I was life. I was Being. I was the vibrant force that filled
the room, and was the room. I was the world, the universe. I
was everything. I was that which always was and always would
be. I was Jim, and Jim was me, and we were everybody else; and
everybody else was us, and all of us put together were the same
thing, and that same thing was the only thing there was. We
were not God. We were simply all that there was, and all that
there was wasn't God. It was us, alone. And we were each other,

and nowhere anywhere was there anything else but us, and we were always the same, the one and only truth.

"Jim," I said, "can you get me out of this?"

"Uh-huh. You want to try it another half-hour?"

"Yes," I said. "Let's try it another half-hour."

Having been reunited with the Ground of my Being, I wanted urgently to be estranged from it again as quickly as possible. But I tried to hold on, at least for a while, and I tried to laugh at the terrifying idea that was building up in my mind. "I don't want to be God," I said. "I don't even want to be city editor." But it did no good to laugh, and I stopped trying. Of course I wasn't God, I knew that. But I was All That There Was, and I didn't want to be that, either. It was dark now, and I could hear children playing somewhere outside the hospital— under a street lamp, no doubt—and their lonely voices filled me with sadness. *The children,* I thought. The children, and Jim, and me: we were all the God there was. And it was sad and awful, because I wanted there to be a God. For the children at least, if not for me. But the loss of God was not the worst of it; there was something far worse even than that. The loss of my little self was not the worst of it; nor indeed did I regret that at all. It was not what I had lost. It was what I had gained. I had gained the whole universe, it seemed, and that was more than I could cope with—more than I could bear.

I didn't want it.

But who was I, who didn't want it? I was Everybody, the Self. And now I knew what the little selves were for, I thought. They were a fiction designed to protect the Self from the knowledge of its own Being—to keep the Self from going mad. For surely, without them, the Self might be driven to insanity by the thought of its own audacity, and the thought of its loneliness, and the thought as well of the danger it was in. And it *was* in danger, I knew that perfectly well. Since it was All That There Was, there was nothing to assure it of its own immortality. And in fact, I could sense, there was that which resisted both its Being and Becoming. And this something was nothing more than Nothingness itself, against which the Self had exerted its will to Become. Thus the ontic anxiety, as Tillich expressed it: the ultimate fear of ultimate non-Being. Or so it seemed, as I struggled with my seven demons; and translating the Self into selves once more, I imagined that I now understood with perfect clarity the meaning of a passage that had always haunted me in Unamuno's story of the good priest Don Emmanuel. That saintly man had preached to his flock the word of God and the message of salvation, which gave them great joy. There were those, however, who perceived that Don Emmanuel himself was a tormented soul, and one day, while walking in the countryside, a villager named Lazarus begged the priest to tell him the truth—the truth above all! And all a-tremble, Don Emmanuel whispered into the ear of him who had asked: "The truth? The truth, Lazarus, is perhaps something so unbearable, so terrible, something so deadly, that simple people could not live with it!"

Now I thought that I knew this truth: the deadly and unbearable truth that *nobody created us . . . we created ourselves.* That was the horror that we could not live with, I thought— anything rather than that—and I raved to Jim: "Tell the truth now, Jim. There is no God, is there? Oh God. It's awfully hard. Why does life have to be so hard? Why can't everything be nice? Oh God . . . God. I don't want life to be *this* way. Oh God, I can't face this. I'm not ready. I'm not ready. I don't have what it takes. I don't have the courage to meet it."

Jim said: "It's an illusion we build up from the time we're little kids. We don't often encounter—"

Shut up! "It's too soon, too soon. Too soon, I tell you. Oh God, we're not supposed to look at this. Not now. Maybe in a million years, or a billion years, or ten billion years. But not now, not yet. It was wrong to do this. The drug . . . not right . . . we shouldn't be fooling with . . ." My voice trailed off, and I thought about Freud. I thought that Freud didn't know what he was talking about, and the unconscious was very simple, really: the unconscious was this knowledge I now had of ultimate Being, and our repressions of it had their roots in an existential terror, not neurosis. It was real, and it was horrifying. It was more than most of us could accept, and thus we took refuge in smaller identities and well-defined roles, creating a limited world we could comfortably live in, pretending all the time there was Something Else. But there was nothing else, and deep down inside us we knew it, and we suffered. It took courage to Be, just as Tillich said, and most of us didn't have that courage. So we rejected our Being—and not by killing ourselves, because death was impossible, but by denying our real identity. By refusing to face what we actually were.

"Jim," I said, "we're all there is."

"That's right, buddy boy."

"God, you're tough. You don't look it, but you're really tough. I just wish that I . . . Jim . . . Can you get me out of this?"

"Sure. Want to try another half-hour first?"

"All right. Another half-hour."

All That There Was. But even this—*even this*—was not the

worst of it. I said that I was frightened by what I had gained, and this was true. But I had lost something, too, and it was more important to me than my wretched self, and more important even than God. For along with my own self I had lost all the other selves as well. I had lost other people. And I missed them very much.

I wanted there to be someone else. Anyone else. And if there had been just two of us—really two of us—and we two were All That There Was, that would not have been so hard. But there was no one else; there was only the One.

Sitting in that room, I could hear church bells ringing some-where, a long way off, and I imagined that they were Christmas bells. I thought of the holiday season, and the crowds thronging the downtown streets in the winter night, and the stores all aglow like boxes of light. Snow falling, and carols playing on the loudspeakers. And everyone with a home to go to, and someone there to meet him, and maybe to love him. But *someone else,* in any case. I was not feeling sentimental about Christmas as such; I was thinking rather about the crowds of people—all of them real, all of them different. And I missed them so, the people. More than myself, more than God, more than anything.

It wasn't right, I thought.

"Jim," I said, "get me out of this."

So he got the Thorazine, and he got me out of it. And the doctors let me go home, where there was someone to meet me.

"I'm not going to hurt anybody," I said. "I'm just going to hurt."

I did, too, for several days. Then the mood wore off, and I went back to the world I knew, and I worked in it. Sometimes I would catch glimpses of that different world I had seen in the hospital room, and I would wonder if the experience was going to start all over again. But it never did. There was only one time, when I was flying alone in a little airplane, high over the Illinois prairie. Shut up in the cabin, I felt suddenly trapped and afraid, and more alone than I cared to be. But I dropped down out of the clouds to a lower altitude, and I opened a window, and the feeling passed.

Looking back on the experience, I recall several things. For one, I never forgot that I was under the influence of a drug. For another, I was never wholly convinced that the drug's revelations were true; even during the best moments and worst moments, a part of me warned that the truth might lie elsewhere, and I suppose this was my reporter's instinct expressing itself. For example, the monistic phase might well have been initiated by my momentary panic when Jim left me alone in the room. And my pre-experience reading could perhaps explain my failure to detect any hint of a transcendent reality. Also, I remember a persistent conviction that the experience itself was wrong. Not false, necessarily, but wrong. For some unguessed reason, I felt, it would be better for us not to seek the experience, at least at this time. And finally, whether my phantoms were real or unreal, I regret my cowardice in the face of them: I have the feeling somehow that they might have appeared much friendlier had it been in my power really to confront them.

I include this epilogue simply as an item of interest, if it is, and certainly not as a testament. Obviously there were too many unknown factors involved to draw any conclusions from the experience, and for my part I have not drawn any conclusions. Nevertheless, and just the same, it is something to think about. I shall think about it for the rest of my life.

Index

INDEX

Church, Western (cont'd.)
127, 133, 169; and Bishop
Robinson, 152–154; Bonhoeffer's view of, 150, 173; concern
of, 111–114; Eastern heresies,
79; function of, 114–116; and
mysticism, 110–115; reform of,
173–174; relevance of, 165–
166, 172–174; secularization
of, 150–151, 157, 165. See also
Religion; Theology.
Churches, psychedelic, 117–118,
213–214; and legislation, 118
Cinematographical fallacy, 198
Clear Light of the Void. See Void,
Clear Light of the.
Cognition: Being, 181–182, 187;
deficiency, 181; primary process, 183
Cohen, Dr. Sidney, 29, 41, 44,
200
Confessions of an English Opium
Eater (De Quincey), 69–72
Conscience, 180, 188
Consciousness, 98, 116, 224, 226;
and LSD, 31, 50; mystic, 110;
psychedelic church view of,
118; rational, 220–221; reli-
gious, 57
Cosmos, 89, 98, 132; goal-di-
rected, 219; and man, 18
Cox, Harvey, 155, 165, 173, 174,
193

Darwin, 218; Darwinian trans-
formism, 220
Death, 190, 204–209, 212, 241.
See also Immortality.
Deism, 121–122, 129
Demiurge, 78–79, 83; myth of,
89, 201, 218, 228. See also
Ulysses.

Demythologization, 139–141,
150; of Bible, 126; of Christ,
140–141; of Christianity, 185–
186; of the East, 201–204,
218; of God, 130, 165; methods of, 127
De Quincey, Thomas, 69, 72, 74;
Confessions, 69–72
Determinism, 190, 193, 220, 223
Dharmakaya, laws in, 185
Ding-an-Sich. See Thing-in-itself.
Donne, John, 82
Doors of Perception, The (Huxley), 103–104
Drug experience. See Psychedelic
experience.
Drug movement, 25, 30, 49, 55,
67, 76, 86, 98, 100, 102, 104–
105, 182, 189, 193, 196, 213–
214, 217, 227; and church, 19,
58; dangers of, 24; direction of,
17, 58; Eastern influence, 18,
19, 24, 68, 105–110, 176; and
immanence, 120; implications
of, 22; legislation of, 28; and
mystical experience, 153; religion of, 17, 117–119, 213–
214; and Tibetan Book of the
Dead, 78. See also LSD; Psychedelic.
Drugs, 42, 119; Oriental connotations, 107
Dualism, 64, 82, 93, 211; concepts of, 120; Eastern, 79;
idealism, 49–52 passim, 63;
origin of, 35, 51; perception of,
34, 65; Quietist's view of, 112

East-West synthesis, 18, 25, 69–
89 passim, 90–105 passim,
119–124, 204
Eastern movement, 18–19, 105–

246

A Note on the Author

William Braden was born in Evanston, Illinois, and studied at the Medill School of Journalism at Northwestern University, where he received a Master's degree in 1953. Since 1956 he has been a reporter for the *Chicago Sun-Times* and has written on a wide variety of subjects. For *The Private Sea*, Mr. Braden did not rely on library research; instead he utilized newspaper techniques—talking with key persons in the drug movement, conversing at length with Robinson and Alltzer, among others, and participating in a psychedelic experience. He asked tough questions and combined the answers with his solid understanding of theology and philosophy. Mr. Braden's many prizes include the Marshall Field Award for Distinguished Reporting. He lives in Dundee, Illinois, with his wife, Beatrice, and their two daughters, Anne and Jennifer.